VERIFICATION OF SYSTEMS AND CIRCUITS USING LOTOS, PETRI NETS, AND CCS

VERIFICATION OF SYSTEMS AND CIRCUITS USING LOTOS, PETRI NETS, AND CCS

BY

Michael Yoeli and Rakefet Kol
Technion—Israel Institute of Technology
Haifa, Israel

A JOHN WILEY & SONS, INC., PUBLICATION

Published by John Wiley & Sons, Inc., Hoboken, New Jersey.
Published simultaneously in Canada.

For general information on our other products and services please contact our Customer Care Department within the U.S. at 877-762-2974, outside the U. S. at 317-572-3993 or fax 317-572-4002.

Wiley also publishes it books in variety of electronic formats. Some content that appears in print, however, may not be available in electronic format.

Library of Congress Cataloging-in-Publication Data:
   Yoeli, Michael, 1917-
   Verification of systems and circuits using LOTOS, Petri Nets, and CCS / Michael Yoeli & Rakefet Kol.
        p. cm. — (Wiley series on parallel and distributed computing)
      Includes index.
      ISBN 978-0-471-70449-2 (cloth)
   1. Integrated circuits—Verification.   2. Computer software—Verification.
   3. LOTOS (Computer program language) 4. Petri nets. I. Kol, Rakefet. II. Title.
      TK7874.58.Y64 2008
      621.3815′48—dc22
                                                                                    2007033487

Printed in the United States of America

10 9 8 7 6 5 4 3 2 1

To my spouse Nehama, with thanks for her persistent and helpful encouragement.

Michael

To my family, with endless love.

Rakefet

CONTENTS

## CHAPTER 1

Introduction

Many present-day industrial hardware systems are of considerable complexity. Great efforts are required to produce such systems correctly at reasonable cost and within an acceptable time limit.

To achieve the above goals, it is important to detect design errors at an early stage, and particularly prior to the production process. The correction of design errors that have infiltrated the production process is very expensive and time-consuming.

In view of the above considerations, "formal verification" plays an important role. The purpose of formal verification is to ensure that the intended hardware design (the implementation) indeed meets the requirements of a given functional specification. Throughout this book, relevant concepts of formal verification will be discussed and made precise.

A number of publications have provided an introduction to some important aspects of formal verification. In particular, we refer the reader to References 1–5.

This book presents yet another approach to hardware verification. It deals with the verification of a wide selection of systems and circuits, and applies powerful toolsets for this purpose (see Section 1.4). It originates from the earlier work of Yoeli (6), who provided a step-by-step introduction to digital circuit verification. This book offers an introduction to the formal verification of combinational, iterative, synchronous, and asynchronous circuits. It also presents some valuable insight into approaching basic theorem-proving, the high-level specification language LOTOS (language of temporal ordering specifications), and the elements of Petri nets and the related software tool PETRIFY.

Throughout the book, you will be challenged with questions and exercises for self practicing. Solutions to selected problems are provided in a section preceding the Reference section.

Verification of Systems and Circuits Using LOTOS, Petri Nets, and CCS, by
Michael Yoeli and Rakefet Kol
Copyright © 2008 John Wiley & Sons, Inc.

The book is unique in that it combines a number of powerful theory-based toolsets with an approach to hardware specifications and implementations founded on an "event-based" approach.

1.1 EVENT-BASED APPROACH

The greater part of this text deals with system specifications and descriptions using an event-based approach, rather than a level-based approach. Here "event" refers to an action of the system or its environment, which may be considered to be instantaneous; that is, its duration is negligible. In the case of actions that take some time, we consider the event of starting the action and the event of terminating the action.

In the event-based approach, circuits and systems are specified and described by means of instantaneous events, which could be inputs, outputs, or internal (non-observable) events.

1.2 EVENT-BASED SYSTEMS

In this book we will discuss several systems that are preferably specified and described using the event-based approach. Examples of such circuits and systems include:

(1) Asynchronous circuits, i.e., sequential circuits without global clock control. Typical relevant events are the up- and down-transitions of inputs and outputs. For details, see Chapter 7.
(2) Communication protocols. Of interest are the instantaneous actions "put", "get", "send", and "receive", related to the handling of messages in such protocols. For details, see Chapter 8.
(3) Arbiters. Typical events are the requesting and granting of access to a shared resource. For details, see Chapter 9.

Obviously, there are other examples of circuits and systems that are not covered in this text; these include "synchronous" circuits (i.e., sequential circuits controlled by a global clock) and arithmetic units (e.g., adders and multipliers). These examples are well covered elsewhere as, for example, in (3).

1.3 TYPES OF VERIFICATION

We distinguish between two major types of verification. The first type, which we refer to as "realization", is concerned with relating behavioral specifications to the actual implementation of the relevant system or circuit. For details, see, e.g., Section 7.9, where various concepts of realization are discussed. The second type of verification, which we refer to as "properties verification", is intended to show that a given system satisfies certain essential properties. For example, we verify that a particular arbiter design never enables the simultaneous access of two processes to a shared resource (see Chapter 9). As another example, consider communications over unreliable communication channels. In Chapter 8 we verify that properly designed protocols are capable of transmitting reliable messages over unreliable channels, assuming suitable conditions.

1.4 TOOLSETS USED

One outstanding feature of this text is the extensive use of three different theories of communicating and concurrent processes, namely LOTOS and its associated toolset CADP (see Chapter 4), Petri nets and their related toolset PETRIFY (see Chapter 5), and CCS (Calculus of Communication Systems) and its toolset CWB (Concurrency Workbench) (see Chapter 6). Suitable introductions to the relevant theories and their related toolsets are provided in Chapters 4–6. Chapter 4 deals both with Basic LOTOS, restricted to control aspects only, and with Full LOTOS, which also deals with the handling of data.

1.5 LEVEL-BASED APPROACH

Whereas the major part of this book deals with the above event-based approach, a small part nevertheless illustrates a level-based approach. The well-known level-based approach is widely used in connection with the specification and description of combinational circuits, synchronous (i.e., clock-controlled) circuits, logic–arithmetic units, and many others.

In this book we are mainly concerned with the specification and analysis of combinational circuits (i.e., digital circuits without memory), such as AND-gates and OR-gates. Their inputs and outputs are assumed to be two-valued, either logic-0 and logic-1, or (alternatively) FALSE and TRUE. For details, see Sections 3.6, 4.9, and 10.1.

1.6 OVERVIEW OF THE BOOK

In Section 1.4 we reviewed the contents of Chapters 4–6. The following is a short review of Chapters 2, 3, and 7–11.

In Chapter 2 we introduce the concept of "process", which plays a fundamental role in connection with event-based systems. Stated informally, the important feature of a (non-trivial) process is its capability to perform some (instantaneous) action and consequently evolve into some other process. We are interested in methods of composing processes from simpler ones, as well as in the comparison of different processes.

In Chapter 3 we use the material of Chapter 2 to provide some insight into formal verification of systems and circuits, prior to the presentation of relevant theories and related toolsets (as described in Section 1.4). Section 3.6 summarizes concepts of propositional logic, with which the reader is assumed to be familiar, in preparation for a study of logic gates in Chapters 4 and 10 (as explained in Section 1.5).

In Chapter 7 we apply the toolsets introduced in Chapters 4–6 to the formal, precisely defined verification of asynchronous circuits, i.e., sequential circuits that operate without a global clock. The concept of "realization" plays an important role. We say that a hardware design (an "implementation") "realizes" a given behavior specification if the design indeed "behaves" as specified. Various approaches to this concept of "realization" are formalized and illustrated, using the toolsets of Chapters 4–6.

In Chapter 8 we are concerned with the verification of communication protocols. As mentioned in Section 1.3, the type of communication protocols that we consider are intended to provide reliable point-to-point communication over channels that may be unreliable. Starting with simple protocols over reliable channels, we discuss variants of the "alternating-bit protocol" and provide suitable proofs that these protocols are capable of "overcoming" the problems of a large class of unreliable channels. This chapter makes extensive use of the material of Chapter 4 (LOTOS/CADP).

In Chapter 9 we deal with the verification of arbiters. Arbiters are intended to regulate the access of two or more processes to a single, shared resource, ensuring that at any time only one of the competing processes may gain access to the shared resource. Various strategies are discussed and proven correct, using each of the three toolsets introduced in Chapters 4–6.

In Chapter 10 we discuss a number of additional verification case studies, illustrating again the application of the verification tools of Chapters 4–6. In particular, we discuss pipeline controllers (Section 10.2), producer–consumer systems (Section 10.3), transition counters (Section 10.5), and advanced vending machines (Section 10.6). In Section 10.1 we continue the discussion of logic gates that was started in Section 4.9.

In Chapter 11 we provide recommendations for further studies, including a powerful extension of the concept of Petri nets, and examples of large systems, such as telecommunication systems, that can be verified using the methods described in this book.

1.7   REFERENCES

1. Gupta A. Formal hardware verification methods: a survey. J Formal Meth Syst Design 1992;1:151–238.
2. Kern C, Greenstreet MR. Formal verification in hardware design: a survey. ACM Trans Design Autom Electron Syst 1999;4(2):123–93.
3. Kropf T. Introduction to formal hardware verification. Springer, 1999.
4. Melham T. Higher order logic and hardware verification. Cambridge University Press, 1993.
5. Yoeli M, editor. Formal verification of hardware design. IEEE Computer Society Press, 1990.
6. Yoeli M. Introduction to digital circuit verification. Computer Science Department Technical Report CS-2001-10, Technion, Israel, March 2001. Available at http://www.cs.technion.ac.il/tech-reports/.

## CHAPTER 2

Processes

2.1 INTRODUCTION

In this text we are mainly interested in the specification and description of systems such as communication protocols, asynchronous circuits, pipeline controllers, vending machines, and others that are suitably described using the "event-based" approach (see Chapter 1). We will use the notion of *process* for the purpose of modeling the behavior of such event-based systems. Most processes described in this chapter are related to systems with inputs and outputs. In the next section we relate processes to behavior patterns and discuss some examples of processes as well as some basic concepts.

2.2 EXAMPLES OF PROCESSES AND BASIC CONCEPTS

Example 2.1 (VM1)   This example deals with a coffee-vending machine **VM1** (1) that will accept a coin, dispense a cup of coffee, and will then do nothing further. Its behavior pattern consists of two events occurring sequentially (one after the other). The first event, named '**coin**', refers to "inserting a coin into the coffee-vending machine." The second event is named '**coffee**', and refers to "getting a cup of coffee." The behavior pattern we have in mind (denoted **VM1**) may be specified as follows:

$$\textbf{VM1} := \textbf{ coin;(coffee; \$)}$$

Here we use the symbol ':=' to mean "is defined by." The symbol '$' denotes the trivial behavior of doing nothing. Following LOTOS (see Chapter 4), we will refer to the symbol ';' as a *prefix operator*. An expression such as X;Y is admissible **only** if X is an event and Y is a behavior pattern. If this is the case, then X;Y is to be interpreted as the behavior pattern "event X, followed

Verification of Systems and Circuits Using LOTOS, Petri Nets, and CCS, by
Michael Yoeli and Rakefet Kol
Copyright © 2008 John Wiley & Sons, Inc.

immediately by the behavior pattern Y." Thus, **coffee;$** should be understood as the event **coffee** (which we defined as getting a cup of coffee), followed by the behavior pattern **$**, which means doing nothing. **coin;(coffee;$)** should be understood as the event **coin** (which we defined as inserting a coin into the coffee-vending machine) followed by the behavior pattern **coffee;$**, described above.

Henceforth we prefer to use the term '*process*' to refer to a behavior pattern, properly specified by the means discussed in this chapter.

If **P** and **Q** are processes, and **b** is some event, the statement **P:=b;Q** thus means that **P** is a process that starts with the event **b**, followed by the behavior specified by process **Q**. If **a** is another event, the process **a;P** can be written as **a;(b;Q)** We will write (by convention) **a;b;Q** instead of **a;(b;Q)**. Using the above convention, we may now replace the above definition of **VM1** by

$$\textbf{VM1} := \textbf{coin;coffee;\$}$$

Recall that '**$**' denotes a process and not an event!

Let us now define the following process (which is a subprocess of **VM1**, in the evident sense):

$$\textbf{VM1a} := \textbf{coffee; \$}$$

The following equation evidently follows from the above definitions:

$$\textbf{VM1} = \textbf{coin;VM1a}$$

Note the use of the '=' symbol in the above equation. Thus, it is an equation, and not a definition.

Given a process **P**, we wish to distinguish between events of **P**, which are observable by an outside observer, and events that are *internal*, i.e., are not observable from outside the process **P**. We denote the set of observable actions/events, which the process **P** will eventually engage in, by **Act(P)**. For example, **Act(VM1) = {coin,coffee}**. Note that in the examples discussed in Sections 2.2–2.6 below, all the process events are observable. Internal events will play a role starting in Section 2.7.

For more information about the prefix operator, see Section 2.3. For additional representations of vending machines, see Section 2.6, as well as Section 1.1 of Reference 1.

Example 2.2 (clock) As an example of a simple never-ending process, we consider an (old-fashioned) clock that ticks forever (and this is all we are concerned with). This process may be defined informally as follows:

$$\textbf{clock} := \textbf{tick;tick;tick;...}$$

The above informal three-dot notation (**...**) may be replaced by the following *recursive definition*:

$$\mathbf{clock := tick;clock}$$

Now consider the equation

$$\mathbf{X = tick;X}$$

where **tick** is an event and **X** is an unknown process. This equation can be solved for the unknown process **X**. Hoare (1) teaches how to treat such equations. It can be proven that the above equation **X = tick;X** has a unique solution, which corresponds informally to the above definitions for **clock**. For details, see Section 2.8 of Reference 1.

Consider now a recursive definition **proc := seq;proc**, where **proc** is a process name and **seq** is a finite sequence of events. It is frequently convenient to replace such a recursive definition by the following "star-notation": **proc :=*[seq]**, where the star symbol is to be interpreted as "repeat forever." Thus, the process **clock** may alternatively be defined by

$$\mathbf{clock := *[tick]}$$

Example 2.3 (PBL)   We now turn to a process specifying a never-ending input–output system.
Consider a light that is controlled (switched on and off) by means of a push button. Let **push?** denote the activation of the push button, let **on!** denote the changing of the light from 'off' to 'on', and let **off!** denote its changing back to 'off'. The '?' symbol is not part of the name of the event, but rather a suffix that may optionally be used to emphasize that an event is an input event. Similarly the '!' suffix is used to indicate an action (output event) produced by the process under consideration. If we assume that this button–light system never fails, and that it starts with the light being off, its *behavior* may be described by the process **PBL**, with the input event **push?** and the output events **on!** and **off!**.

This process **PBL** may be specified informally by the following infinite repetitive sequence of events, where the three dots **...** (as in Example 2.2) indicate "repeat forever":

$$\mathbf{PBL := push?;on!;push?;off!;push?;on!;push?;off!;...}$$

Formally, this process may be specified by the following *recursive definition*:

$$\mathbf{PBL := push?;on!;push?;off!;PBL}$$

Or as

$$\textbf{PBL} := \textbf{push;on;push;off;PBL}$$

This definition is based on the fact that after the first occurrence of the sequence **push?;on!;push?;off!;** the system returns to its initial state.

Alternatively, we may use the star-notation (as in Example 2.2), and define PBL as

$$\textbf{PBL} := \textbf{*[push?; on!; push?; off!]}$$

The notation introduced in this chapter, which we will refer to as *Blot*, is a simplified version of the standard notation of *Basic LOTOS*, which will be introduced in Chapter 4.

2.3   ABOUT PREFIXING

We have already introduced (in Section 2.2) the prefix operator ';'.

Note that $\textbf{P} = \textbf{a;Q}$ implies that **a** is the one and only event that **P** is capable of engaging in. Note furthermore that $\textbf{P} = \textbf{a;Q}$ implies that **P** is uniquely determined, given **Q** and **a**.

This is summarized in the following law, wherein we informally use the equals symbol '=', to mean "specify the same event or behavior." A more formal definition is presented in Section 2.7.

Law 2.1: $\textbf{a;P} = \textbf{b;Q}$ iff $\textbf{a} = \textbf{b}$ and $\textbf{P} = \textbf{Q}$

The following law is rather evident:

Law 2.2: $\textbf{*[a;b]} = \textbf{a;*[b;a]}$

This law also holds if **a** and **b** are replaced by finite sequences of events.

2.4   PROCESS GRAPHS

Processes may also be represented by so-called process graphs. They are similar to state graphs representing finite automata. Both state graphs and process graphs are directed graphs, the arcs of which are labeled by events. However, whereas the nodes of state graphs represent states, the nodes of a process graph **PG**, representing the process **P**, represent the processes

$$a;b;c;\$ \xrightarrow{a} b;c;\$ \xrightarrow{b} c;\$ \xrightarrow{c} \$$$

Figure 2.1   Process graph of the process **a;b;c;$**.

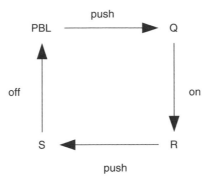

Figure 2.2   Process graph of the process **PBL**.

reachable from **P** by a sequence of actions. The graph **PG** is rooted and its root represents the process **P** itself. A labeled arc of a process graph from a node v1 to a node v2 represents a feasible transition from process **P1** to process **P2**, where process **Pj** is represented by node vj.

For example, the process **a;b;c;$** is represented by the process graph of Fig. 2.1. Figure 2.1 can also be viewed as a state graph representing a finite automaton. The states in this state graph have unconventional labels: the root node is labeled **a;b;c;$**, the following state is labeled **b;c;$**, and so on.

The process graph representing the process **PBL** from Section 2.2 is shown in Fig. 2.2, in which the processes are defined as **PBL:=push;Q**, **Q:=on;R**, **R:=push;S**, and **S:=off;PBL**.

2.5 CHOICE OPERATOR

Using only the operators ';' and '*', introduced so far, we are restricted to behaviors that can be represented by a single sequence (finite or infinite) of events. However, we are frequently interested in behaviors represented by a choice between different event sequences. Hence we now introduce the *choice operator* '[ ]'.

To illustrate the usage of the choice operator, consider a vending machine **VM2** that, once a coin is inserted, lets you choose between receiving coffee and receiving tea. Specifically, this vending machine has a "coffee" button and a "tea" button. After you insert the coin, you should press one of these two buttons, and the machine will output the corresponding drink. Vending machine **VM2** may be specified by the following behavior expression:

VM2 := coin;CM2

CM2 := coffee;$ [ ] tea;$

coffee := press_coffee_button;get_coffee_drink

tea := press_tea_button; get_tea_drink

where '[ ]' is the above choice operator. Similar to **VM1**, this machine also functions only once.

Alternatively, this vending machine can be represented by the process graph of Fig. 2.3. For simplicity, we have omitted the details of the compound events **coffee** and **tea** in this figure, and we view them as a single (compound) event.

The notation **P[a > Q** will be used to indicate that **a** is one of the events **P** is capable of performing, and that, after engaging in the event **a**, the process **P** behaves as specified by process **Q**. Thus, in the above example, **CM2[coffee > $** and **CM2[tea > $**. This means that process **CM2** may engage in the (compound) event **coffee**, or it may engage in the compound event **tea**. In both cases it will reach the null process **$**.

Stated generally, let **P1** and **P2** be processes. Their choice **P1 [ ] P2** defines the process **P**, which may behave either as **P1** or as **P2**. Thus, **P** may be defined as follows:

1. If **P1[x > R1**, then **P1 [ ] P2[x > R1**
2. If **P2[y > R2**, then **P1 [ ] P2[y > R2**

Note If **P1[x > R1** and **P2[x > R2**, then **P1 [ ] P2[x > R1** as well as **P1 [ ] P2 [x > R2**.

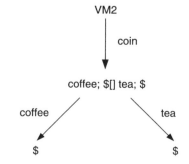

Figure 2.3 Process graph of **VM2**.

We emphasize that the choice operator [ ] applies to processes, and not to events! Therefore the construct **(a [ ] b);$** is not admissible, but **a;$ [ ] b;$** is.

2.6 ANOTHER PROCESS EXAMPLE

Vending machines have been used extensively by Hoare (1) to illustrate processes. Our process examples introduced so far are modified versions of Hoare's machines.

Example 2.4 (VM3)   This is another modification of one of Hoare's vending machines, proposed by Milner (2):

> **Act(VM3) = {in1p, in2p, big, little, collect}**
>
> **VM3 : = in2p;big;collect;VM3 [ ] in1p;little;collect;VM3**

Here the customer may either insert a 2p coin, order and collect a big chocolate, or insert a 1p coin, then order and collect a little chocolate.

2.7 EQUIVALENCES

Recall the distinction between events that are observable by an outside observer and events that are not observable (introduced in Section 2.2). Following Basic LOTOS (which is discussed in Chapter 4), we shall be concerned with a unique non-observable event, denoted 'i'. We wish to clarify under which conditions two processes may appear equivalent to an outside observer, although they may differ, as far as internal events are concerned. It is convenient to use process graphs for the formal definitions of process equivalences.

2.7.1 Strong Equivalence

First we define *strong equivalence*. Two processes are *strongly equivalent* iff every event (observable or not) of one process can be matched by the same event in the other process, such that the outcomes are again strongly equivalent.

Stated more formally, let **GP** and **GQ** be process graphs, corresponding to processes **P** and **Q**, respectively. A relation R between the node sets of **GP** and **GQ** is a strong equivalence between **P** and **Q** if the following conditions are satisfied:

(i)   The roots of **GP** and **GQ** are R-related.

(ii)   If pRq and p[a > p' in **GP** (i.e., there exists an arc in **GP** from p to p' labeled by 'a'), then there exists a node q' in **GQ**, such that q[a > q' and p'Rq'.

(iii)   If pRq and q[a > q' in **GQ**, then there exists a node p' in **GP**, such that p[a > p' and p'Rq'.

Note   If in the above definition, condition (iii) is omitted, we say that process **P** is a *strong preorder* of process **Q**, or process **Q** is a *strong cover* of process **P**.

It is noteworthy that the above concept of "strong cover" of processes corresponds to the concept of "weak homomorphism" between automata, as defined in References 3 and 4.

We use the equality symbol '=' to denote strong equivalence.

The following is an example illustrating strong equivalence:

$$\textbf{a;b;\$ = a;(b; \$ [ ] b;\$)}$$

Note that we have already used '=' to indicate that two processes have the same behavior, which may now be formalized to mean "are strongly equivalent."

2.7.2   Observation Equivalence

We now turn to the definition of *observation equivalence* (cf. Milner (2)). Let **a** be any observable event of some process. We call an *extension* of **a** any sequence in **i*ai***, where **i*** is any finite sequence of zero or more **i**'s.

Two processes are called *observation-equivalent* if any extension of an observable event in one process can be matched by some extension of the same observable event in the other process, and the outcomes are again observation-equivalent. Furthermore, if two processes are observation-equivalent, they should remain so after an 'i' event occurs in one of them.

This "definition" of observation equivalence can easily be stated formally, following our above formal definition of strong equivalence. Furthermore, the preceding definitions of "strong preorder" and "strong cover" are related to "observational preorder" and "observational cover" in a rather evident way.

Example 2.5   The processes **i;a;i;i;b;\$** and **a;i;b;\$** are observation-equivalent, but are not strongly equivalent.

Example 2.6   Let **P1 = a;(b;\$ [ ] c;\$)** and **P2 = a;b;\$ [ ] a;c;\$**. It is important to realize that the two processes are not observation-equivalent. Namely, if both processes perform the action **a**, **P1** changes into **b;\$ [ ] c;\$**, whereas **P2** becomes either **b;\$** or **c;\$**. Thus, the outcomes are no longer observation-equivalent. On the other hand, the two processes coincide with respect to their feasible event sequences, which are **a**, **ab**, and **ac**. Therefore the two processes are *trace-equivalent.*

Example 2.7 Let **P1 = a;$ [ ] b;$** and **P2 = i;a;$ [ ] b;$**. Here **P2** may perform the internal action **i**, and become **a;$**. No corresponding action is possible in **P1**. In view of the last sentence of our above definition of observation-equivalence, the two processes are not observation-equivalent. However, the two processes are again trace-equivalent.

For closely related definitions of observation equivalence, see References 2 and 5.

2.7.3 Some Additional Laws

The following laws "evidently" apply to the choice operator; we use '=' to indicate strong equivalence:

<u>**Law 2.3:**</u>	**P [ ] P = P**
<u>**Law 2.4:**</u>	**P [ ] Q = Q [ ] P**
<u>**Law 2.5:**</u>	**(P [ ] Q) [ ] R = P [ ] (Q [ ] R)**

2.8 LABELED TRANSITION SYSTEMS (LTSs)

In this section we introduce labeled transition systems (cf. Milner (2)) and show how they are related to finite state machines as well as to processes.

A *Labeled Transition System* is a 4-tuple $S = (Q,A,T,q0)$, where

- Q is a finite, nonempty set of states
- A is a finite, nonempty set of labels (denoting actions)
- T (the transition relation) is a subset of $Q \times A \times Q$
- q0 is the initial state

A finite, non-deterministic state machine is defined similarly, but there, A is the set of inputs and outputs.

We now point out our way of describing LTSs. In conformity with CADP (see Chapter 4), we let $Q = \{0, 1, \ldots, k\}$ and $q0 = 0$. We will specify an LTS by listing all elements of its transition relation. Figure 2.4 shows two examples of LTS specifications.

The above definitions of strong and observation equivalence also apply to LTSs in the evident sense, with "process" replaced by "state". We may also define equivalences between an LTS and a process, as illustrated below.

The *LTS2.1* in Fig. 2.4 may be viewed as strongly equivalent to the process **a;b;$**. Similarly, we consider the *LTS2.2* from Fig. 2.4 to be strongly equivalent to the process **a;b;$ [ ] a;c;$**. Here state 3 corresponds to $, state 1 to the process **b;$**, and state 2 to the process **c;$**.

```
                          (0,a,1)
                          (0,a,2)
           (0,a,1)        (1,b,3)
           (1,b,2)        (2,c,3)


           LTS2.1        LTS2.2
```

Figure 2.4   Labeled transition systems *LTS2.1* and *LTS2.2*.

2.9 PARALLEL OPERATORS

2.9.1 Parallel Composition

There are several ways to compose processes to form a larger process. One important method is that of *parallel composition.*

As a simple example, consider the two processes (specifying event sequences) **P** = a;b;c;$ and **Q** = d;b;e;$. In their parallel composition, denoted **P ‖ Q** (using Blot notation), they *synchronize* (i.e., they perform simultaneously) on any observable action shared by the two processes. In the above example, the only shared observable action is evidently **b**. Hence the two processes **P** and **Q** will perform action **b** concurrently, provided both processes are ready to do so. Actions not shared by the two processes will be performed in **P ‖ Q** as specified by each process separately. Thus

$$\textbf{P} \parallel \textbf{Q} = a;d;b;c;e;\$[\ ]a;d;b;e;c;\$[\ ]d;a;b;c;e;\$[\ ]d;a;b;e;c;\$$$

Note that in the parallel composition of processes, the processes do not synchronize on the non-observable action **i**; e.g., **a;i;b;$ ‖ i;a;i;b;$** = **i;a;i;i;b;$**. In the next section we provide a formal definition of the Blot version of the parallel composition operator.

2.9.2 Synchronization Operator ‖ (Blot Version)

Let **P** and **Q** be processes and let L denote all the observable events that the two processes have in common. We define their *parallel composition* **P ‖ Q** as follows:

(1) If P[a > P' and a is not in L, then P ‖ Q[a > P' ‖ Q.
(2) If Q[b > Q' and b is not in L, then P ‖ Q[b > P ‖ Q'.
(3) If P[c > P' and Q[c > Q', where c is in L (i.e., the event c is observable and common), then P ‖ Q[c > P' ‖ Q'.
(4) If P[i > P', then P ‖ Q[i > P' ‖ Q.
(5) If Q[i > Q', then P ‖ Q[i > P ‖ Q'.

(6) If none of the above cases is applicable to $P \| Q$, then the composition $P \| Q$ forms a *deadlock*, i.e., this parallel composition is "stuck" and is unable to perform any action (see Example 2.9 below). In general, a deadlock is undesirable, and it indicates some flaw in the design.

Note If cases (4) and (5) are both applicable, they may be applied one after the other, in any order (see Example 2.10 below).

2.9.3 Examples of Parallel Compositions

Example 2.8 Let $P = a;b;c;\$$ and $Q = b;d;\$$. Then

$$P \| Q = a;(b;c;\$ \| b;d;\$) \qquad \{by\ (1)\}$$

$$= a;b;(c;\$ \| d;\$) \qquad \{by\ (3)\}$$

$$= a;b;(c;d;\$ [\ ] d;c;\$) \qquad \{by\ (1)\ and\ (2)\}$$

Example 2.9 Let **syn2** $= a;b;\$ \| a;b;a;\$$. This process will encounter a deadlock state, after performing the sequence **a;b**. Using Blot notation, we may state that the process **syn2** equals **a;b;stop**.

Example 2.10 Let $P = i;a;P'$ and $Q = i;a;Q'$. Then

$$P \| Q[i > a;P' \| Q[i > a;P' \| a;Q'[a > P' \| Q' \qquad \{by\ (4)\ and\ (5)\}$$

Alternatively,

$$P \| Q[i > P \| a;Q'\ [i > a;P' \| a;Q'[a > P' \| Q' \qquad \{by\ (5)\ and\ (4)\}$$

Thus

$$P \| Q = i;i;a;(P' \| Q').$$

2.9.4 More Laws

The following is a suitably modified version of some of the material in Section 2.3 of Reference 1. The laws listed below follow easily from the definition of Section 2.9.2 above. In the following, let **a** be an observable action not in **Act(Q)**, let **b** be an observable action not in **Act(P)**, and let **c** be an observable action shared by the processes **c;P** and **c;Q**. Here are some simple relevant laws (recall that we use '=' to denote strong equivalence).

Law 2.6:	$P \| Q = Q \| P$
Law 2.7:	$(P \| Q) \| R = P \| (Q \| R)$
Law 2.8:	$c;P \| c;Q = c;(P \| Q)$

Law 2.9:   a;P ‖ b;Q = a;(P ‖ b;Q) [ ] b;(a;P ‖ Q)
Law 2.10:   a;P ‖ Q = a;(P ‖ Q)

2.9.5 Sample Proof

Using the laws introduced so far, let us prove that

$$*[c;a] \, \| \, *[b;c] = b;c;(\, *[a;c] \, \| \, *[b;c])$$

Proof

$$*[c;a] \, \| \, *[b;c] =$$

= *[c;a] ‖ b;*[c;b]   {applying Law 2.2}

= b;(*[c;a] ‖ *[c;b])   {applying Laws 2.6 and 2.10}

= b;c;(*[a;c] ‖ *[b;c])   {applying Laws 2.2 and 2.8}

2.9.6 Interleaving Operator |||

If **P** and **Q** are processes, then **P** ||| **Q** represents their parallel execution without any "synchronization," i.e., each process proceeds independently of the other. Using Blot, we have, for example,

$$a;b;\$ \, ||| \, c;\$ = c;a;b;\$ \, [\,] \, a;c;b;\$ \, [\,] \, a;b;c;\$$$

where '=' again denotes strong equivalence.

2.10 SEQUENTIAL COMPOSITION

Let **P** be a process that terminates properly (i.e., a process without deadlock) and let **Q** be some other process. We introduce the Blot notation (adapted from LOTOS) **P ≫ Q** to denote their *sequential composition*. **P ≫ Q** is obtained from **P** by replacing all occurrences of '$' in **P** by **i;Q**.

Example 2.11   Let **P** = a;b;$ ‖ b;c;$ and **Q** = d;$. Then **P ≫ Q** = a;b;i;d;$ ‖ b;c;i;d;$. Thus **P ≫ Q** and a;b;c;d;$ are observation-equivalent.

EXERCISES

2.1   Let **EX2.1** = *[a;b] [] *[c;d]. Construct the relevant process graph. *Hint*: In a process graph, a label may appear more than once.

2.2 Let **EX2.2 = (a;*[b;c]) [] *[c;d]**. Design the corresponding process graph.

2.3 Look at the process COPYBIT specified in Reference 1, p. 31. Rewrite this specification using the notation introduced in this chapter.

The following three exercises illustrate how the Blot operator '‖' can be eliminated.

2.4 Prove the following equivalence:

$$*[a;c] \| *[b; c] = *[a;b;c [] b;a;c]$$

Here **P = *[seq1 [] seq2]** is defined by **P = seq1;P [] seq2;P**, where **seq1** and **seq2** are finite sequences of actions. Recall, however, that **[seq1 [] seq2]**, standing alone (i.e., without the preceding star) is not defined! *Hint*: use a similar approach to the example in Section 2.9.5.

2.5 Let **P = *[a;c]**, **Q = *[c;b]**. Transform **P ‖ Q** into an expression without a parallel operator. *Hint:* see, e.g., Reference. 1, p. 71.

2.6 Let **P = *[a;b]**, **Q = *[b;c]**, **R = *[a;c]** Transform **(P ‖ Q) ‖ R** into an expression without parallel operators.

2.7 Simplify the expression **a;b;c;$ ‖ (a;b;c;$ [] a;c;$)**.

2.11 FURTHER READING

If you wish to read an alternative introduction to processes, formulated in a very friendly, popular style, we recommend that you look at pages 23–31 of Reference 1. An attractive feature of this introduction is the illustration of the concept of processes by means of vending machines, dispensing tea, coffee, chocolates, and cookies, some of which we introduced in the preceding sections. Reference 1 is the standard introduction to a CSP (communicating sequential processes)-based analysis of systems. There are some differences between the CSP-based notation and ours, which is oriented towards LOTOS (see Chapter 4), rather than CSP.

In particular, CSP uses '→' instead of our symbol ';' and '**STOP**' (usually with subscripts) instead of our **$**. Note also that our star (*) notation is easily eliminated. For example, **P0 = *[a;b]** can be replaced by **P0 = a;b;P0**. Similarly, the CSP μ-operator is also easily eliminated. For example, let **P = μX.F(X)**, then **P** satisfies the recursive equation **P = F(P)**. Considering the above specification of process **P0**, we may also write **P0 = μX.a;b;X**. Finally, the CSP symbol '|' is related to our choice symbol '[ ]', but there are some differences!

2.12 SELECTED SOLUTIONS

2.1   See Fig. 2.5.

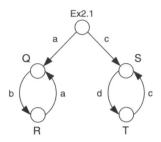

Figure 2.5   Process graph solution of Exercise 2.1.

2.2   See Fig. 2.6.

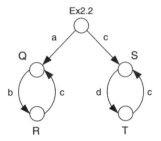

Figure 2.6   Process graph solution of Exercise 2.2.

2.3   COPYBIT = in.0;out.0;COPYBIT [ ] in.1;out.1;COPYBIT.

2.4   Here is a shortened version of the required proof:

> **Q = *[a;c] || *[b;c]**
>
>   **= a;*[c;a] || b; *[c;b]**
>
>   **= a;b;(*[c;a] || *[c;b]) [ ] b;a;(*[c;a] || *[c;b])**
>
>   **= a;b;(c;*[a;c] || c;*[b;c]) [ ] b;a;(c;*[a;c] || c;*[b;c])**
>
>   **= a;b;c;(*[a;c] || *[b;c]) [ ] b;a;c;(*[a;c] || *[b;c])**
>
>   **= a;b;c;Q [ ] b;a;c;Q**

2.5   Similar to the example of Section 2.9.5, we get **P || Q = a;c;(*[a;c] || *[b;c])**. And now we apply Exercise 2.4.

2.6 By applying the rules of Section 2.9.4, we easily obtain

$$(P \| Q) \| R = a;b;c;((P \| Q) \| R) = *[a;b;c]$$

2.7 a;b;c;$ [ ] a;stop.

2.13 REFERENCES

1. Hoare CAR. Communicating sequential processes. Prentice-Hall, 1985.
2. Milner R. Communication and concurrency. Prentice-Hall, 1989.
3. Ginzburg A, Yoeli M. Products of automata and the problem of covering. Trans Am Math Soc 1965;116:253–66.
4. Yoeli M. Generalized cascade decompositions of automata. J ACM 1965; 12(3):411–22.
5. Bruns G. Distributed systems analysis with CCS. Prentice-Hall, 1996.

## CHAPTER 3

From Digital Hardware to Processes

In accordance with our event-based approach, we use processes (see Chapter 2) to represent specifications as well as implementations. For the purpose of verification, we use the toolsets listed in Section 1.4. This chapter is intended to introduce our verification approach, prior to the application of the above toolsets.

3.1 THE C-ELEMENT

In this section we review various hardware components, which will play an important role in the sequel. The C-Element (or CEL-circuit) is an example of such a component. It was introduced originally by D.E. Muller (1), and is frequently referred to as the "Muller C-Element." It is *sequential*, i.e., it has a memory and its output is not uniquely determined by its current inputs.

3.1.1 The 2-Input CEL-Circuit

The 2-input CEL-circuit has two binary inputs (ranging over 0 and 1), namely A and B, and one binary output Z. The circuit is stable iff $A \neq B$ or $A = B = Z$. A circuit is *stable* iff its output will not change as long as its inputs do not change. Assuming that the initial conditions are $A = B = Z$, its event-based (*dynamic*) behavior is represented by the following Blot expression:

$$CEL[a,b,z] = CEL = a;b;z;CEL \ [\ ] \ b;a;z;CEL$$

Here (and later on) we use lower-case letters to denote a transition (both up and down) of the input or output denoted by the corresponding upper-case letter. If we wish to distinguish between the two types of transitions, we use, e.g., $A+$ to denote an up-transition of A, and $A-$ to denote a down-transition.

Verification of Systems and Circuits Using LOTOS, Petri Nets, and CCS, by Michael Yoeli and Rakefet Kol

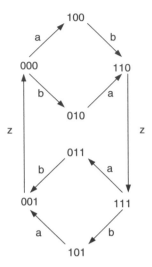

Figure 3.1   State/event diagram of **CEL[a,b,z]**.

Starting from the initial state $A = B = Z = 0$ (abbreviated to 000), a feasible sequence of states and events is, e.g., <000, **a**, 100, **b**, 110, **z**, 111, **a**, 011, **b**, 001, **z**, 000>.

A complete state/event diagram of the CEL-circuit is shown in Fig. 3.1 (we assume that an input may change only if the circuit is stable!).

The CEL-circuit has a similar function to a SET–RESET flip–flop. The SET command is $A = B = 1$ and the RESET command is $A = B = 0$.

The CEL-circuit may be realized by means of a MAJORITY-gate implementing the Boolean function $Z <=> ((A \wedge B) \vee (A \wedge C) \vee (B \wedge C))$ (also known as the full-adder carry-out function). In a MAJORITY-gate the output is evidently determined by the majority of the input values. A CEL-circuit can be obtained from a MAJORITY-gate by providing a feedback connection from Z to the input C, which consequently is no longer an independent input.

The CEL-circuit may also be specified by the Blot expression

$$\mathbf{CEL1} = {}^*\mathbf{[a;z]} \parallel {}^*\mathbf{[b;z]}$$

EXERCISE

3.1   Prove that **CEL1 = CEL**, i.e., that the processes CEL and CEL1 are strongly equivalent.

3.1.2 The 3-Input CEL-Circuit

The above definition of a (2-input) CEL-circuit is easily extended to more than 2 inputs. A 3-input CEL-circuit may be implemented as shown in Fig. 3.2. It has the binary inputs A, B, C and the binary output Z. Y represents an internal connection. The block diagram of the circuit shown in Fig. 3.2 may be described by the following expression:

$$\textbf{CEL3[A,B,C,Z]} = \textbf{(CEL[A,B,Y] \,|[Y]|\, CEL[Y,C,Z]) \textbackslash \{Y\}}$$

Here |[Y]| indicates that Y is an internal connection between the two CEL-circuits; namely, the output Y of the first CEL-circuit becomes an input to the second CEL-circuit. The notation \{Y} indicates that Y is to be considered an internal (non-observable) connection.

The required behavior of the CEL3-circuit may be specified by the Blot expression

$$\textbf{cel3spec} = \textbf{*[a;z] || *[b;z] || *[c;z]}$$

This specification assumes that the circuit is started in one of the initial states A = B = C = Z. One easily verifies that the above specification can be transformed into

cel3spec1 = a;b;c;z;cel3spec1 [] a;c;b;z;cel3spec1 [] ... [] c;b;a;z;cel3spec1

We now claim that the circuit shown in Fig. 3.2 "satisfies" the specification **cel3spec1**. This statement is to be interpreted as follows. If the environment of the circuit shown in Fig. 3.2 behaves in accordance with the specification **cel3spec1**, the resulting output will also be in accordance with the specification. Informally, this statement is easily verified. Starting, for example, from the initial state A = B = C = Y = Z = 0, and changing all inputs from 0 to 1, in any order, the output Z will also change to 1.

On the other hand, the implementation of Fig. 3.2 is more powerful than the specification. For example, the implementation, starting from the above

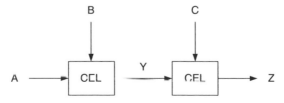

Figure 3.2 Block diagram of **CEL3**.

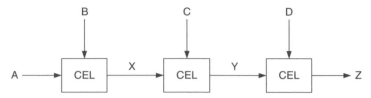

Figure 3.3   Block diagram of **CEL4**.

all-zero initial state, is capable of executing the sequence <**a,b,y,a**>, but this behavior is not part of the specification.

The above statement, its precise formulation, and its formal proof will be taken up again in Chapter 7, using the theories and toolsets that are introduced in Chapters 4–6.

3.1.3   The 4-Input CEL-Circuit

The preceding considerations are easily extended to k-input CEL-circuits. For example, 4-input CEL-circuits may be implemented by using three 2-input CEL-circuits, as shown in Fig. 3.3. The relevant specification becomes

$$\textbf{cel4spec} = \textbf{*[a;z]} \parallel \textbf{*[b;z]} \parallel \textbf{*[c;z]} \parallel \textbf{*[d;z]}$$

The corresponding verification problem will be dealt with formally in Chapter 7.

3.2   THE XOR-GATE

3.2.1   The 2-Input XOR-Gate

A 2-input XOR-gate is a combinational circuit with binary inputs A and B and a binary output Z. The circuit is stable iff A $\neq$ B and Z = 1, or A = B and Z = 0. The level-based analysis of k-input ($k > 1$) XOR-gates is straightforward (cf. Section 10.1). However, in the context of our event-based approach, we will treat k-input XOR-gates similarly to the k-input CEL-circuits discussed in Section 3.1. The above (2-input) XOR-gate may be specified as follows (assuming the gate is stable):

$$\textbf{A\#B = Z, where 0\#0 = 1\#1 = 0, and 0\#1 = 1\#0 = 1}$$

Evidently, if (logical) 1 is replaced by the truth value T (true), and (logical) 0 is replaced by F (false), the above XOR-operator '#' represents the logical connective **xor** (= **exclusive or**).

We now assume that the environment of this XOR-gate is restricted in the following way:

(i) An input may change only if the gate is stable.

(ii) Only one input may change at any given time.

Regarding restriction (i), if $A = B = Z = 1$, then the gate is unstable and Z has the tendency to change. Assume that this output change from 1 to 0 occurs fast enough, before a change of input A (from 1 to 0) becomes effective. Since $(0\#1) = 1$, this input change will restore the output to 1. Thus a short 0-pulse may occur. In asynchronous circuits such pulses may interfere with the correct operation of the circuit, and should be prevented.

Regarding restriction (ii), you can easily verify that in a case where both inputs are changed together in some stable state, one input change may become effective quickly and the other slowly. This may again lead to a short detrimental output pulse.

The admissible state transitions may be summarized as follows:

(1) If the state is stable, then each of the input changes **a** and **b** are applicable; the resulting state will be unstable.

(2) If the state is unstable, then only an output change **z** may occur; the resulting state is stable.

The corresponding state/event and state-set/event diagrams of an XOR-gate are shown in Fig. 3.4.

Using Blot, we may represent the behavior of the above XOR gate, started at any one of its stable states, as follows:

$$\textbf{XOR[a,b,z] = XOR = a;z;XOR [] b;z;XOR}$$

Thus, starting in any of its stable states, the XOR-module may engage in any of the two event sequences **a;z** and **b;z**, and the outcome will again be a stable state. Viewed as an "asynchronous module," i.e., as a basic building block of asynchronous circuits, this gate is also referred to as **2-MERGE** or simply as **MERGE** (see Reference 2).

3.2.2 The 3-Input XOR-Gate

A 3-input XOR-gate is easily constructed, similar to the construction of the 3-input CEL-circuit (Fig. 3.2). The block diagram of a 3-input XOR-gate is shown in Fig. 3.5. Its level-based analysis is straightforward (see Section 10.1). However, here we are again concerned with its application as an

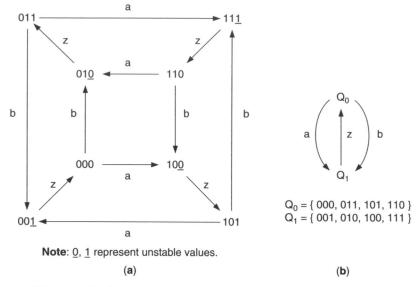

Note: 0, 1 represent unstable values.

(a)   (b)

Figure 3.4   Event (**a**) and state-set (**b**) diagrams of **XOR[a,b,z]**.

event-based module. In this connection, we formulate the following Blot specification:

$$\textbf{xor3spec} = \textbf{a;z;xor3spec [] b;z;xor3spec [] c;z;xor3spec}$$

The block diagram of Fig. 3.5 may be described, similar to the above description of **CEL3[A,B,C,Z]**, as

$$\textbf{XOR3[A,B,C,Z]} = (\textbf{XOR[A,B,Y] } |[\textbf{Y}]| \textbf{ XOR[Y,C,Z]}) \setminus \{\textbf{Y}\}$$

In Chapter 7 we will formulate precisely the following statement and will provide a proof of it:

XOR3[A,B,C,Z] is a realization of xor3spec

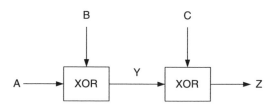

Figure 3.5   Block diagram of **XOR3**.

3.3 TOGGLES

Toggles are additional building blocks, applicable to the design of event-based systems and circuits. We first consider a 1-input, 2-output toggle device (**TOG**).

Let A be its input, and Y, Z its outputs, as shown in Fig. 3.6. The behavior of **TOG** may be represented by the state/event diagram shown in Fig. 3.7. The hardware design of such a toggle device is well covered in most introductions to basic logic design. Using Blot, the behavior of **TOG** may be summarized as follows:

$$\textbf{tog[a?,y!,z!] = *[a;y;a;z]}$$

This specification assumes that the module is started in the initial "all-zero" condition, i.e., $A = Y = Z = 0$. Here we use '?' to indicate an input and '!' to denote an output.

A 1-input 4-output toggle **TOG4** may be specified similarly. Namely,

$$\textbf{tog4.spec[a?,w!,x!,y!,z!] = *[a;w;a;x;a;y;a;z]}$$

Such a "4-toggle" may be implemented using three **TOG** modules, as shown in Fig. 3.8. The verification of this 4-output toggle example is straightforward.

The case of a 3-toggle is more interesting: a 3-toggle may be derived from a 4-output toggle by the addition of an XOR-module. The corresponding block diagram is shown in Fig. 3.9. We will return to this 3-toggle verification example in Section 7.5.

We will present a more formal discussion of k-output toggles in Section 10.5.

Figure 3.6   TOG[A,Y,Z].

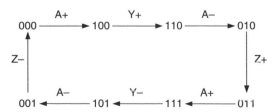

Figure 3.7   State/event diagram of the toggle device **TOG[A,Y,Z]**.

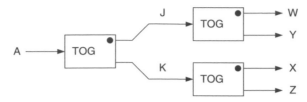

Figure 3.8   Block diagram of 4-toggle (**TOG4**).

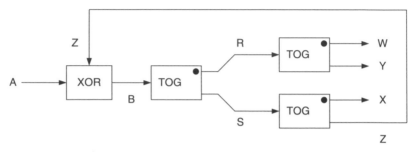

Figure 3.9   Block diagram of 3-toggle (**TOG3**).

3.4 MODULO-*N* TRANSITION COUNTERS

3.4.1 Modulo-*N* Transition Counter Specification

A modulo-*N* transition counter has one binary input A and two binary outputs Y and Z. For $N = 3$, the behavior of this counter may be specified as follows:

$$\textbf{cnt3[a,y,z] = cnt3.spec[a,y,z] = *[a;y;a;y;a;z]}$$

Here we assume that the counter is started in the state $A = Y = Z = 0$.

For any value of N ($N > 1$), the behavior of the modulo-*N* transition counter may be specified as follows:

$$\textbf{cntN[a,y,z] = cntN.spec[a,y,z] = *[(a;y)**(N--1);a;z]}$$

We use $\textbf{w}^{**}\textbf{N}$ to denote the sequential repetition of w, *N* times. Furthermore, we again assume that the counter is started in the above "all-zero" state.

3.4.2 Modulo-*N* Transition Counter Implementations

Most of the following material is based on Ebergen and Peters (3). Also refer to Reference 2.

3.4.2.1 The Cases N = 3 and N = 4 The implementation of the modulo-3 transition counter specified above (**cnt3.spec[a,y,z]**) can immediately be derived from the implementation of the 3-toggle (**TOG3**), indicated in Fig. 3.9. All that is required is the replacement of outputs W, X, Y by Y, Y, Z, respectively. A transition on the output Z indicates that three transitions were counted (the Y-outputs are irrelevant).

Similarly, the implementation of a modulo-4 transition counter can be derived from Fig. 3.8 by simply changing the outputs W and X to Y.

3.4.2.2 The N > 4 Case In accordance with Reference 3, the modulo-N transition counter, where N is even and $N > 2$, can be decomposed into a modulo-$N/2$ counter, a toggle, and an XOR-gate, as shown in Fig. 3.10. For odd values of N, $N > 4$, the decomposition shown in Fig. 3.11 is applicable.

You can easily verify examples of the above design approaches with step-by-step simulation.

For a more formal discussion of modulo-N counters, see Section 10.5.

3.5 MODULAR NETWORKS

In this section we deal with compositions (networks) of the modules introduced in Sections 3.1 and 3.2.

Example 3.1 Consider the network shown in Fig. 3.12. We claim that this network "satisfies" the following Blot specification:

$$\textbf{cct3\_12.spec} = *[((a;\$ \; [] \; b;\$) \; \| \; c;\$ \; \| \; d;\$) \gg z;\$]$$

A formal approach to the concept of "satisfies" is presented in Section 7.7. In the meantime, you may use again a step-by-step simulation to partially verify the above claim. For example, try to apply the sequence **<b;d;c>** to the

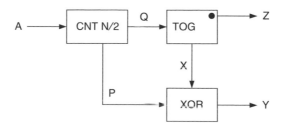

Figure 3.10 Decomposition of modulo-N transition counter; N even, $N > 2$.

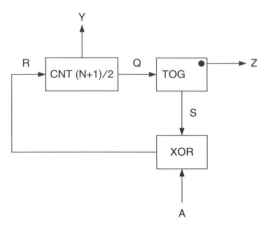

Figure 3.11   Decomposition of modulo-N transition counter; N odd.

network of Fig. 3.12, assuming the "all-zero" initial state. You will easily confirm that the outcome of this sequence is Z+, and that the value of Z remains 0 until then.

Example 3.2   Consider the network shown in Fig. 3.13. This network (**CXC.imp**) can be described as follows, using Blot:

$$\textbf{CXC.imp} = ((\textbf{CEL[a,b,y1]} ~ ||| ~ \textbf{CEL[c,d,y2]}) ~ || ~ \textbf{XOR[y1,y2,z]}) \setminus \{\textbf{y1,y2}\}$$

The intended behavior specification may be formulated as follows:

$$\textbf{CXC.spec} = *((\textbf{a;\$} ~ || ~ \textbf{b;\$}) ~ [] ~ (\textbf{c;\$} ~ || ~ \textbf{d;\$})) \gg \textbf{z;\$})$$

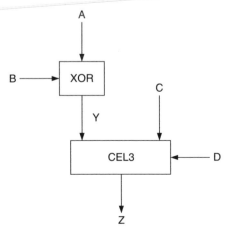

Figure 3.12   Network of **cct3_12.spec** = *[((a;\$ [] b;\$) || c;\$ || d;\$) ≫ z;\$].

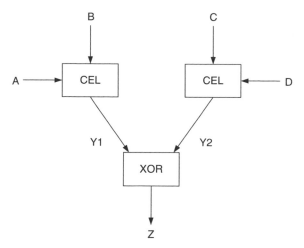

Figure 3.13   Network **CXC.imp**.

To "verify" informally that the above network **CXC.imp** indeed satisfies the above specification, we point out that the specification requires the network to be capable of performing any one of the four event sequences, starting from an admissible initial state, and returning back to such a state, as described by

$$a;b;z, b;a;z, c;d;z, d;c;z$$

EXERCISE

3.2   Determine the relevant initial states of the above **CXC.imp** network, and use a step-by-step simulation to verify the above satisfaction claim. We shall return to this example in Section 10.4 and provide a formal verification for it.

3.6 PROPOSITIONAL LOGIC: A REVIEW OF KNOWN CONCEPTS

As indicated, we are mainly concerned with systems and circuits that are preferably dealt with using the event-based approach, rather than the level-based approach. Nevertheless, a rather small part of our text will also deal with the level-based approach, in particular in connection with "combinational" circuits. In a combinational circuit the present output depends only on the present inputs, i.e., such a circuit has no memory.

An essential tool for the specification and description of combinational circuits is the part of formal logic known as *propositional*. In this section we summarize the basic concepts relevant to propositional logic. We assume familiarity with the basics of propositional logic. This section is mainly intended to establish our relevant approach and the notation to be used in the sequel. In Sections 4.9 and 10.1 we illustrate the application of LOTOS (see Chapter 4) to the verification of combinational circuits.

3.6.1   Logical Operators

A *proposition* is a statement that is either true or false. We say that a true proposition has the *truth value* T (true) and a false proposition has the truth value F (false). Thus any given proposition has a unique truth value. One can construct *compound propositions* from given propositions by means of *logical operators*. The truth value of a compound proposition is uniquely determined by the truth values of its constituent propositions.

If p and q are propositions, then the (compound) proposition $p \wedge q$ (p AND q) is true iff (if and only if) both p and q are true. Thus the proposition $(2 > 1) \wedge (0 + 0 = 0)$ is true, whereas $(1 > 2) \wedge (0 + 0 = 0)$ is false.

Evidently, the propositions $p \wedge q$ and $q \wedge p$ are *equivalent*, in the sense that they always have the same truth value, whatever the truth values of p and q may be. We will write $f = g$ to state that the (compound) propositions f and g are equivalent in this sense, i.e., they are *logically equivalent*.

The usual way of defining a logical operator, such as $\wedge$, is by means of a *truth table*. For the operator $\wedge$, we have the following truth table:

p	q	$p \wedge q$
F	F	F
F	T	F
T	F	F
T	T	T

The proposition $p \vee q$ (p OR q) is false iff both p and q are false. In other words, $p \vee q$ is true iff p is true or q is true or both p and q are true. Thus the proposition $(1 > 0) \vee (0 > 2)$ is true, and so is $(1 > 0) \vee (2 > 0)$. The corresponding truth table becomes

p	q	$p \vee q$
F	F	F
F	T	T
T	F	T
T	T	T

The proposition $\sim p$ (NOT p) is true iff p is false.

3.6.2 Proving Logical Equivalences

A straightforward way to prove equivalences of propositions, as defined above, is by means of truth tables. Namely, for each distribution of truth values we compute the resulting truth values of both sides of the given equivalence. A slightly more advanced approach is a proof "by cases."

To illustrate this approach, we first establish the following equivalences:

E1.a: $p \wedge T = p$ **E1.b:** $T \wedge p = p$

E2.a: $p \wedge F = F$ **E2.b:** $F \wedge p = F$

E3.a: $p \vee T = T$ **E3.b:** $T \vee p = T$

E4.a: $p \vee F = p$ **E4.b:** $F \vee p = p$

Let us now prove the equivalence $p \wedge (q \vee r) = (p \wedge q) \vee (p \wedge r)$. We proceed by considering the two cases $p = T$ and $p = F$.

Case p = T

$\qquad$ LHS $= q \vee r$ {by E1.b}

$\qquad$ RHS $= q \vee r$ {by E1.b, applied twice}

Case p = F

$\qquad$ LHS $= F$ {by E2.b}

$\qquad$ RHS $= F \vee F$ {by E2.b}

$\qquad\qquad = F$ {by E4.a}

We now list various additional properties (equivalences) of the operators $\wedge$ and $\vee$; they are all easily proven by means of the truth-table approach or the above "proof by cases" method:

E5.a: $p \wedge p = p$ **E5.b:** $p \vee p = p$

E6.a: $p \wedge q = q \wedge p$ **E6.b:** $p \vee q = q \vee p$
$\qquad$(commutativity)

E7.a: $(p \wedge q) \wedge r = p \wedge (q \wedge r)$ **E7.b:** $(p \vee q) \vee r = p \vee (q \vee r)$
$\qquad$(associativity)

E8.a: $p \wedge (q \vee r) = (p \wedge q) \vee (p \wedge r)$ **E8.b:** $p \vee (q \wedge r) = (p \vee q) \wedge (p \vee r)$
$\qquad$(distributivity)

E9.a: $\sim (p \wedge q) = \sim p \vee \sim q$ **E9.b:** $\sim (p \vee q) = \sim p \wedge \sim q$

Note that from a mathematician's point of view we may regard p, q, r above simply as Boolean variables, i.e., variables ranging over the domain {F, T}. The operators ∧, ∨, ∼ are defined on this domain as shown by the above truth tables.

EXERCISE

3.3 Use the "proof by cases" method to verify the above equivalences E7.a and E8.b. Does the efficiency of the proof depend on the appropriate choice of the case variables?

3.6.3 Tautologies and the EQUIV Operator

A compound proposition is a *tautology* iff it is always true, i.e., for every possible distribution of truth values. Examples of tautologies are

$$p \vee \sim p, \ (p \wedge q) \vee (\sim p \vee \sim q)$$

We may convert every logical equivalence into a tautology by replacing the logical equivalence symbol (=) by the **EQUIV** operator <=> defined as follows: p <=> q is true iff either both p and q are true or both p and q are false. Thus we get the following truth table:

p	q	p <=> q
F	F	T
F	T	F
T	F	F
T	T	T

Examples of tautologies derived by the above method are

$$(p \wedge q) <=> (q \wedge p)$$

$$(p \wedge q) <=> \sim(\sim p \vee \sim q)$$

Another logical operator of interest is the **IMPL** (implication) operator =>. The proposition p => q is false iff p is true but q is false.

3.7 SELECTED SOLUTIONS

3.1 See the solution of Exercise 2.4.

3.3. Proving equivalence E7.a:

Case p = T

$$LHS = (T \wedge q) \wedge r = q \wedge r$$

$$RHS = T \wedge (q \wedge r) = q \wedge r$$

Case p = F

$$LHS = (F \wedge q) \wedge r = F \wedge r = F$$

$$RHS = F \wedge (q \wedge r) = F$$

Proving equivalence E8.b:

Case p = T

$$LHS = T \vee (q \wedge r) = T$$

$$RHS = (T \vee q) \wedge (T \vee r) = T \wedge T = T$$

Case p = F

$$LHS = F \vee (q \wedge r) = q \wedge r$$

$$RHS = (F \vee q) \wedge (F \vee r) = q \wedge r$$

You will easily verify that the efficiency of the above proofs does depend on the choice of the case variables.

3.8 REFERENCES

1. Muller DE. A theory of asynchronous circuits. Technical Report 66, Digital Computer Laboratory, University of Illinois, Urbana-Champaign, December 1955.
2. Encyclopedia of Delay-Insensitive Systems (EDIS), November 1998. http://edis.win.tue.nl/.
3. Ebergen JC, Peters AMG. Modulo-N counters. In: Staunstrup J, Sharp R, editors. Designing correct circuits. Elsevier; 1992. p. 27–46.

## CHAPTER 4

Introducing LOTOS

In this chapter we introduce an important approach to digital systems and circuits, based on *LOTOS* and the associated toolbox *CADP*. LOTOS (Language Of Temporal Ordering Specification) is a high-level specification language originally intended for the specification and verification of communication protocols. However, LOTOS is also applicable to discrete systems, particularly parallel, event-based systems, as well as to digital circuits, and particularly to modular asynchronous circuits. CADP (1) is a powerful toolset, developed at the INRIA Institute in Grenoble, France.

CADP now stands for "Construction and Analysis of Distributed Processes". Originally, it stood for "CAESAR/ALDEBARAN Development Package". For further details of CADP, see Section 4.8.

4.1 FROM BLOT TO BASIC LOTOS

In this section we illustrate how Blot specifications may be converted into Basic LOTOS specifications, which can then be analyzed using the CADP toolbox.

Example 4.1 Consider the Blot specification

$$ex4\_1 = a;b;\$ \; [] \; c;d;\$$$

When we wish to convert this Blot specification into a (Basic) LOTOS specification, we have two options as to the way we handle the '$' symbol. The first is to replace the '$' by 'stop'. The second is to replace the '$' by 'exit'. In general, 'stop' refers to an undesirable termination, such as deadlock (to be discussed later on), whereas 'exit' indicates a proper ("successful") termination.

Verification of Systems and Circuits Using LOTOS, Petri Nets, and CCS, by
Michael Yoeli and Rakefet Kol

The following are the corresponding specifications in (Basic) LOTOS:

File ex4_1a.lotos
specification ex4_1a[a,b,c,d]:noexit behaviour
        (a;b;stop) [] (c;d;stop)
endspec

File ex4_1b.lotos
specification ex4_1b[a,b,c,d]:exit behaviour
        (a;b;exit) [] (c;d;exit)
endspec

If two processes are strongly equivalent, we say that they have the same behavior. LOTOS programs, such as the two listed above, specify a behavior by means of a representative process.

The above two LOTOS files specify the behavior of the Blot process **ex4_1**, in accordance with the two options indicated above. The process is described in the second line of each file, with '$' replaced by either 'stop' or by 'exit'. We name the two processes here 'ex4_1a' and 'ex4_1b', respectively. These names appear in the heading (starting with "specification"), together with the (observable) actions involved. The term 'exit' in the heading indicates that the process is properly terminating (no recursion and no deadlock are involved), whereas 'noexit' indicates that the process does not terminate properly (or does not terminate at all).

Henceforth, we will use '$' in Blot to correspond to 'exit' in LOTOS, and will use 'stop' in Blot, the way it is used in LOTOS.

4.1.1   Recursion

Consider the following recursive behavior specification:

$$\text{PUD} = *[\text{up;down}] = \text{up;down;PUD}$$

The following file 'pud.lotos' illustrates how such a recursion is dealt with in LOTOS:

File pud.lotos
specification pud[up,down]:noexit behaviour
        P[up,down]

where
    process P[up,down]:noexit:=
        up;down;P[up,down]
    endproc
endspec

4.2 SOME SEMANTICS

The "meaning" of the various LOTOS operators introduced so far can be derived from the explanations given in Chapter 2 with respect to the related Blot operators. More formally, the semantics ("meaning") of the LOTOS operators discussed so far can be based on the following rules, which will enable us to convert a given LOTOS specification into an LTS (labeled transition system; see Section 2.8).

Rule 4.1:   x;P [x>P

To illustrate this rule, consider the LOTOS expression **X4.1 := a;b;c;stop**. The corresponding LTS may be specified as follows:

$$0 \; [a>1 \; [b>2 \; [c>3$$

Here state **0** represents **X4.1**, and states **1**, **2**, **3** represent processes **b;c;stop**, **c;stop**, and **stop**, respectively.

On the other hand, consider the LOTOS expression **X4.2 := a;b;c;exit**. In this case, the relevant LTS is specified to be

$$0 \; [a>1 \; [b>2 \; [c>3 \; [exit>4$$

Here the additional transition **3[exit>4** indicates that the process **X4.2** terminates properly.

The following two semantic rules apply to the choice operator []:

Rule 4.2(a):   if P[x > P' then P [] Q [x > P'

Rule 4.2(b):   if Q[y > Q' then P [] Q [y > Q'

To illustrate this rule, let **X4.3 :– a;b;stop [] c;d;stop** (specified in the above ex4_1a.lotos file).

The transitions of the corresponding LTS are as follows:

LTS of X4.3

(0,a,1)
(1,b,3)
(0,c,2)
(2,d,3)

We now turn to recursion, where the following rule is applicable:

> **Rule 4.3:** let **P : = E**, where **P** is a process name, and **E** is a process expression. The symbol ':=' denotes "is defined by". Assume **E[x > E'**. Then **P[x >E'**.

To illustrate this rule, consider the recursive definition **PUD := up;down;PUD** (cf. Section 4.1.1). Applying **Rule 4.3**, we get **PUD[up>PUD'**, where **PUD' := down;PUD**. Applying **Rule 4.3** again, we get **PUD'[down >PUD**.

In summary, we get the following LTS derived from the above definition of **PUD**:

LTS of PUD

(0,up,1)
(1,down,0)

4.3 FROM LTS TO LOTOS

It is rather easy to convert a given LTS (see Section 2.8) into an observation-equivalent process. To illustrate, consider the LTS shown in the following file LTS4_1:

File LTS4_1
(0,A,1)
(1,B,0)
(1,C,3)
(0,D,2)
(2,E,3)
(3,F,0)

To obtain an observation-equivalent process, we associate a process with each state, which has more than one incoming transition and/or more than one outgoing transition. The corresponding LOTOS file is as follows:

File lts.lotos
specification lts[a,b,c,d,e,f]:noexit behaviour
      P0[a,b,c,d,e,f]
where
  process P0[a,b,c,d,e,f]:noexit:=
      a;P1[a,b,c,d,e,f] [] d;e;P3[a,b,c,d,e,f]
  endproc
  process P1[a,b,c,d,e,f]:noexit:=
       b;P0[a,b,c,d,e,f] [] c;P3[a,b,c,d,e,f]
  endproc
  process P3[a,b,c,d,e,f]:noexit:=
      f;P0[a,b,c,d,e,f]
  endproc
endspec

Here process Pj represents state 'j' of the above LTS.

4.4 COMPARING PARALLEL OPERATORS

As indicated earlier, Blot is a simplified version of Basic LOTOS. In particular, this is true in connection with the use of parallel operators. The construct **P ‖ Q** is the same in Blot and Basic LOTOS only if **Act(P) = Act(Q)**. If this does not hold and **L** is the set of observable actions common to **P** and **Q**, then we have to write **P|[L]|Q** in Basic LOTOS, if **P** and **Q** are to synchronize on all actions in **L**, whereas we may still write **P ‖ Q** in Blot. More generally, if **L** is any set of observable actions, shared by both **P** and **Q**, the notation **P|[L]|Q** in Basic LOTOS (as well as in Blot) refers to the parallel composition of the two processes, with synchronization on all actions in **L**.

The parallel operators introduced in Chapter 2 are easily incorporated into actual LOTOS programs. As an example, consider the following LOTOS file, which essentially produces the expression ***[a;c]‖ *[b;c]**:

File expar1.lotos
specification expar1[a,b,c]:noexit behaviour
      cycle[a,c] |[c]| cycle[b,c]
where

```
    process cycle[a,b]:noexit:=
        a;b;cycle[a,b]
    endproc
endspec
```

─────────────

4.5 SEQUENTIAL COMPOSITION

In Section 2.10 we introduced the concept of "sequential composition" and illustrated this concept using Blot. Our Blot notation '>>' coincides with the notation used in LOTOS.

The following is a LOTOS file representing the Blot expression

$$\textbf{seqcomp.blot} := \textbf{(a;b;exit} \parallel \textbf{b;c;exit)} \gg \textbf{d;exit}$$

(see Example 2.11):

File seqcomp.lotos
specification seqcomp[a,b,c,d]:exit behaviour
        (a;b;exit |[b]| b;c;exit) >> d;exit
endspec

─────────────

In Exercise 4.7 below we suggest that you compare the above LOTOS file with the Blot expression **a;b;c;d;$**.

4.6 HIDING

The hiding facility of LOTOS allows us to transform some observable actions of a process into non-observable ones. This facility will be illustrated in the following chapters.

4.7 EQUIVALENCES AND PREORDERS

In Chapter 2 we introduced the concepts of strong equivalence and behavioral equivalence. By now you know how to convert a LOTOS program into the corresponding LTS. The equivalence concepts introduced in Chapter 2 can immediately be applied to LTSs. Thus you know how to apply equivalence concepts to processes defined by LOTOS programs. A similar comment applies to the concepts of strong and observation-equivalent preorders.

4.8 ABOUT CADP

At the beginning of this chapter we mentioned CADP, the powerful toolset associated with LOTOS. We will now show you how to actually use CADP.

At this stage, you need to have access to CADP, so that you can actively participate in the development of the material that is about to be presented. See (1) to learn more about CADP, and especially how the CADP package can be obtained. If your Department/Institute does not yet have access to CADP, you will probably need the assistance of an IT system engineer. Together with the CADP package, you should also obtain and become familiar with the relevant parts of the CAESAR and ALDEBARAN tools. For details about these tools, consult the relevant online manuals. In the sequel we will mainly use the two tools CAESAR and ALDEBARAN, with CAESAR usually being combined with ALDEBARAN. Some differences might exist between the version used in this text and the version that you have available.

To learn more about CADP tools, including CAESAR and ALDEBARAN, go to Reference 1, and from there to Tools Overview, Manual Pages, and Publications.

As long as you have problems with obtaining CADP, try to "imitate" CADP as we go along and compare your imitation with the material offered in this chapter.

4.8.1 Getting Started with CADP

To get started with CADP, open a dedicated directory, and copy the above LOTOS file ex4_1a.lotos (from Section 4.1) into this directory. Now issue the following CADP command:

caesar -aldebaran ex4_1a.lotos

The outcome is a file ex4_1a.aut, listing the LTS of the LOTOS expression X4.3 as shown in Section 4.2, together with the heading des(0,4,4).

In general, a heading $(0,j,k)$ of an aut-file indicates that the initial state is 0, the number of the following lines is j, and the number of states is k.

If you replace **ex4_1a** by **ex4_1b** in the above CADP command, you will obtain the following aut-file:

File ex4_1b.aut
des(0,6,6)
(0,a,1)
(0,c,2)
(1,b,3)
(2,d,4)

(3,exit,5)
(4,exit,5)

4.8.2 Verifying Equivalences and Preorders Using CADP

4.8.2.1 Verifying Equivalences Using CADP You may use the command *aldebaran* of CADP to check equivalences between two LTSs. To do so, issue the command *aldebaran* followed by one of the following directives:

-bequ   to compare two LTSs with respect to strong equivalence

-oequ   to compare two LTSs with respect to observation equivalence

To illustrate this, copy the following files into your dedicated directory:

File ex4_2.lotos
specification ex4_2[a,b]:exit behaviour
        a;b;exit
endspec

File ex4_3.lotos
specification ex4_3[a,b]:exit behaviour
        i;a;b;exit
endspec

Now apply the command *caesar-aldebaran* to the preceding two files, in order to get the files ex4_2.aut and ex4_3.aut, respectively.

The processes specified in the files ex4_2.lotos and ex4_3.lotos are evidently observation-equivalent. You may verify this by using the command

aldebaran -oequ ex4_2.aut ex4_3.aut

You will get the outcome 'TRUE'.

However, if you replace *-oequ* by *-bequ*, you will get an explanation why the two processes are not strongly equivalent.

You may also use the command *aldebaran* to reduce a given LTS modulo observation equivalence; that is, to get a minimal LTS, observation-equivalent to the original one. The relevant command is

aldebaran -omin file.aut

For example, if you apply this command to ex4_3.aut, you will get ex4_2.aut (with changed state names).

4.8.2.2 *Verifying Preorders Using CADP* In Section 2.7 we introduced the concepts of strong preorder and observation preorder. We now indicate how these concepts may be applied to recursive LOTOS specifications. For example, consider the following three Blot specifications:

$$xab = a;b;xab$$

$$xabc = a;b;xabc \,[\,] \,a;c;xabc$$

$$xiab = i;a;b;xiab$$

Let *.aut be the corresponding aut-files. Then the following CADP commands will be confirmed to be TRUE:

aldebaran -bord xab .aut xabc .aut

aldebaran -oord xiab .aut xabc .aut

Here **-bord** refers to strong preorder and **-oord** to observation preorder.

4.8.3   Generating LTS of Choice Using CADP

Recall that **P [ ] Q** denotes a process that behaves either like **P** or like **Q**. For example, consider the following LOTOS file 'choice.lotos':

File choice.lotos
specification choice[a,b]:exit behaviour
        (i;a;exit) [ ] (b;exit)
endspec

———————————

Copy this file and generate the relevant choice.aut file (try imitation first!). You should get the following result:

File choice.aut
des(0,4,4)
(0,i,1)
(1,A,2)
(0,B,2)
(2,exit,3)

———————————

4.8.4 Generating LTS of Recursion Using CADP

Consider now the LOTOS file pud.lotos from Section 4.1. We may again use the command

caesar -aldebaran pud.lotos

to derive an LTS from pud.lotos and obtain the corresponding aut-file

File pud.aut
des(0,2,2)
(0,up,1)
(1,down,0)

_____

Lines 2 and 3 of this file clearly coincide with the LTS of PUD constructed in Section 4.2.

EXERCISES

Exercises intended for the actual use of the CADP-package are marked by '@'.

4.1 Consider the Blot expression **a;b;c;$ || d;a;c;$**. Convert this expression into a strongly equivalent Blot expression without parallel operators. @ Confirm your result by using CADP.

4.2 @ Use CADP to convert the above program *lts.lotos* from Section 4.3 into the corresponding aut-file and compare the outcome with the file LTS4_1 (listed also in Section 4.3).

4.3 Let   **PX4_3a = *[a;b] [ ] *[c]**

   PX4_3b = *[a;i;b] [ ] *[c]

  (a) Prove that the two processes are observation-equivalent.
  (b) @ Use CADP for the proof of (a).

4.4 @ Use CADP to show that **i;a;$ [ ] b;$** and **a;$ [ ] b;$** are *not* observation-equivalent. (For a direct proof, see Example 2.7 in Chapter 2.)

4.5 @ Use CADP to prove that ***[a;c] || *[b;c] = *[a;b;c [ ] b;a;c]**. (For a direct proof, see Exercise 2.4.)

4.6   @ Use CADP to transform *[a;c] || *[c;b] into an expression without parallel operators (cf. Exercise 2.5).

4.7   @ Use CADP to show that *seqcomp.lotos*, defined above, and the Blot-expression **a;b;c;d;$** are observation-equivalent. (For a direct proof, see Example 2.11.)

4.9   FULL LOTOS—AN INTRODUCTION

So far, we have been working with Basic LOTOS, suitable for dealing with control structures, but not with data structures. In this section we introduce *Full LOTOS*, which is an extension of Basic LOTOS, and is capable of dealing with both control as well as data structures. In the version that we are working with, Full LOTOS has access to a large library of data types, such as Booleans, Natural Numbers, Integers, and many more. However, in this section we will deal only with the data type "Boolean". We will illustrate the use of the data type "Boolean" by considering digital circuits, which are best specified using the "level-based" approach, rather than the "event-based" approach that we have been using so far. In particular, we will deal with "combinational" circuits, i.e., circuits without memory. We assume familiarity with propositional logic. For a relevant review of concepts assumed to be known, see Section 3.6. For a further discussion of the application of Full LOTOS to the analysis of combinational circuits, see Section 10.1.

4.9.1   The Full-LOTOS NOT-Gate Example

To illustrate the use of Full LOTOS, we consider a level-based NOT-gate, with a Boolean input IN1 and a Boolean output OUT. The gate we consider first will act as an inverter only once. Namely, it will accept a Boolean input on IN1, output $\sim$(IN1) on OUT, and then consider its task as completed. Recall that we use ' $\sim$ ' to denote the logical 'not' operator. Let T and F stand for 'TRUE' and 'FALSE', respectively. Then $\sim$T = F and $\sim$F = T.

4.9.1.1   The Full LOTOS NOT-File   Applying Full LOTOS, such a NOT-gate may be specified by means of the following file:

File NOT0.lotos
specification NOT0[IN1,OUT]: exit
library BOOLEAN endlib
behaviour
        NOT0[IN1,OUT]

where
   process NOT0[IN1,OUT]:exit:=
      IN1 ?x:Bool;
      OUT! not(x);
      exit
   endproc
endspec

The above file has some similarities with Basic-LOTOS files. A major difference is the use of the library BOOLEAN, which enables us to declare variables involved as Boolean. Other libraries of interest available via CADP are BIT, INTEGER, and NATURAL.

The above file NOT0.lotos uses the definition of 'not' provided by the library BOOLEAN. Other Boolean operators defined in the above library are 'and', 'or', 'xor', and 'eq'.

The line "IN1 ?x:Bool" in the above file is to be interpreted as follows:

> "get the Boolean input appearing on the input line IN1 and
>
> assign it to the variable x"

Similarly, the line "OUT! not(x);exit" means the following instruction:

> "output the value of not (x) on the output line OUT;
>
> then terminate this process"

4.9.1.2 Applying CADP to Derive LTS for the NOT-Gate
CADP enables us to derive the following labeled-transition type file *NOT0.aut* from the above *NOT0.lotos* file.

File NOT0.aut
des(0,6,6)
(0, "IN1 !FALSE", 1)
(0, "IN1 !TRUE", 2)
(1, "OUT !TRUE", 3)
(2, "OUT !FALSE", 4)
(3, exit, 5)
(4, exit, 5)

This file is the labeled transition system representing the above LOTOS file in the evident sense.

To derive this aut-file we have to issue the following commands. First, we will run

caesar.adt NOT0.lotos

This command deals with the data part of the given LOTOS file. We may now proceed as in the case of Basic LOTOS, so the next command should be

caesar -aldebaran NOT0.lotos

The outcome of this command is the file NOT0.aut shown above.

4.9.2 The Non-Terminating NOT-Gate

We shall now consider the specification of a conventional, non-terminating NOT-gate. The corresponding LOTOS file is as follows:

File NOT1.lotos
specification NOT1[IN1,OUT]: noexit
library BOOLEAN endlib
behaviour
     NOT1[IN1,OUT]
where
   process NOT1[IN1,OUT]: noexit:=
     IN1 ?x:Bool;
     OUT! not(x);
     NOT1[IN1,OUT]
   endproc
endspec

Proceeding as before, we may use CADP to derive the following file:

File NOT1.aut
des(0,4,3)
(0, "IN1 !FALSE", 1)
(0, "IN1 !TRUE", 2)
(1, "OUT !TRUE", 0)
(2, "OUT !FALSE", 0)

4.9.3   The Max Specifications

4.9.3.1   Max2 Specification   As further illustration of the application of
Full LOTOS, we introduce the data type "NATURAL", which deals with a
wide range of operations on the natural numbers. As an example, we wish
to determine the maximum value of two natural numbers. This is achieved
in the following Max2 specification:

File max2.lotos
specification max2[a,b,c]:noexit
library BOOLEAN, NATURAL endlib
behaviour
      max2[a,b,c]
where
   process max2[a,b,c]:noexit:=
       a?x:nat [x < 3]; b?y:nat [y < 3]; c!max(x,y);
       max2[a,b,c]
   endproc
endspec

————————————

The above file accepts two natural numbers **a** and **b**, and outputs the value
c = max(a,b). The input values of **a** and **b** are assigned to the variables **x** and
y, respectively.

In the above file we restricted the acceptable values of **a** and **b** to the range
$\{0,1,2\}$, simply in order to come up with omin-files of reasonable size. You
may derive this omin-file, by the application of CADP, as illustrated in earlier
examples.

4.9.3.2   Max3 Specification   The above Max2 specification may be
adapted to determine the maximum value of three natural numbers, as illustrated in the following file:

File max3.lotos
specification max3[a,b,c,out]:noexit
library BOOLEAN, NATURAL endlib
behaviour
      max3[a,b,c,out]
where
   process max3[a,b,c,out]:noexit:=
       a?x:nat [x < 3]; b?y:nat [y < 3]; c?z:nat [z < 3];

```
      out! max(x,max(y,z));
      max3[a,b,c,out]
   endproc
endspec
```

Note that this is a simple extension of the above max2 specification. We suggest that you again derive the corresponding omin-file.

For further applications of Full LOTOS to the description of logic gates, see Section 10.1.

4.10 THE REGULAR MU-CALCULUS (RMC)

The mu-calculus (mu = μ) is a powerful tool for expressing and verifying properties of LTSs. For an introduction to the mu-calculus and its application to "model-checking", we recommend the work contained in Reference 2.

In this section we introduce a particular variant of the mu-calculus, namely the "regular mu-calculus" (RMC), which is applicable to verifying LOTOS programs against a variety of properties. This variant of the mu-calculus has been integrated into the CADP toolset, providing an efficient means to verify LOTOS programs against RMC-formulated properties. For an in-depth introduction to RMC, see Reference (3); for a complete users guide, see Reference (4).

4.10.1 Introducing RMC by Examples

In this section we provide an introduction to a rather small subset of RMC, by means of suitable examples.

To start, consider the Blot specification

$$\textbf{test1 = A;B;C; \$ [] D;E;\$}$$

and let *test1.lotos* be the corresponding LOTOS file. We wish to check whether **test1** satisfies the following condition:

check1: " there exists an initial transition followed by (a transition labeled) B "

For this purpose, we set

$$\textbf{check1.mcl := < true > <"B"> true}$$

which is the RMC-based formulation of condition **check1**.

We shall now explain the meaning of the RMC expressions that we are interested in. The "diamond" symbol '$<\ldots>$' is interpreted as "there exists", while the "box" symbol '$[\ldots]$' means "for every". Furthermore, $<$true$>$ means "there exists a transition", whereas [true] means "for every transition".

RMC also makes use of the star operator '*'. For example, $<$true*$>$ is to be understood as "there exists a sequence of transitions (including the empty sequence)". Similarly, $<$true+$>$ refers to non-empty sequences.

In order to state that an RMC expression is true (or false), 'true' (or 'false') is appended to the RMC expression in question.

To check the RMC-property **check1.mcl** against the LOTOS file *test1.lotos*, issue the command

caesar.open test1.lotos evaluator check1.mcl

You will get the output "TRUE".

We suggest that you go to the CADP home page (1) to obtain more details about the **caesar.open** command and about the **evaluator** directive.

The following are a few more mcl-files, together with their informal interpretation and the expected outcome when applied to the *test1.lotos* file, which includes the definition of the above **test1** Blot expression:

check2.mcl := $<$"A"$>$ true

Meaning: there exists an initial transition labeled A.
Outcome: TRUE.

check3.mcl := ["A"] true

Meaning: every initial transition is labeled A.
Outcome: FALSE.

check4.mcl := [(not "A")*] $<$"B"$>$ true

Meaning: B is not necessarily preceded by A.
Outcome: FALSE.

check5.mcl := $<$ true* $><$"C"$>$ true

Meaning: there exists a sequence of transitions followed by C. In other words, C is reachable.
Outcome: TRUE.

check6.mcl := [true*] < true > true

Meaning: every state has a successor state.
Outcome: FALSE.

check7.mcl := [true*] < "A".(not "B")*."C"> true

Meaning: C may follow A without an intervening occurrence of B.
Outcome: FALSE.

EXERCISE

4.8 The following is a Blot specification of a simple arbiter (for more about arbiters, see Chapter 9):

arb0 = R1;G1;D1;A1;arb0 [] R2;G2;D2;A2;arb0

Convert this Blot specification into a proper LOTOS specification. Then formulate and verify the following requirements, using RMC:

(a) Between "G1" and "G2" there must appear "D1".
(b) Initially, "G1" may not appear before "R1".
(c) There is no deadlock.

4.11 FURTHER READING

Reference 5 provides easy additional reading material, dealing with the direct application of Full LOTOS to the specification of small digital circuits. However, it does not establish connections with CADP.

Referece 6 introduces an intermediate specification language, called DILL (Digital Logic in LOTOS), for simplifying the task of applying Full LOTOS to the level-based description of digital circuits.

We recommend that you study the relevant parts of the tutorial in Referece 7. A somewhat more difficult introduction to LOTOS is contained in Reference 8. For further insight into LOTOS and CADP, see (9).

4.12 SELECTED SOLUTIONS

4.1   a;b;c; $ || d;a;c;$ =

d;(a;b;c;$ || a;c;$) =

d;a;(b;c;$ || c;$) =

d;a;b;c;$

You should have no problem confirming the above conversion, using CADP.

4.3 (a)   Both processes may start either with the action **a** or with the action **c**. In both cases the outcomes are clearly observation-equivalent.

   (b)   The following is the file *PX4_3b.lotos*:

File PX4_3b.lotos
specification PX4_3b[a,b,c]:noexit behaviour
        cy3[a,i,b] [] cy1[c]
where
    process cy3[a,b,c]:noexit:=
        a;b;c;cy3[a,b,c]
    endproc
    process cy1[a]:noexit:=
        a;cy1[a]
    endproc
endspec

The file PX4_3a.lotos is designed similarly. Proceed by generating the corresponding aut-files, and verify that they are indeed observation-equivalent.

4.4   Generate the corresponding aut-files and then compare them with respect to observation-equivalence. You should have no problems by now!

4.8   Here are the relevant RMC properties for verifying the requirements in the question:

   (a) [true*."G1".(not "D1")*."G2"] false
   (b) [(not "R1")*."G1"] false
   (c) [true*] < true> true

4.13 REFERENCES

1. CADP Home page, April 2007. http://www.inrialpes.fr/vasy/cadp.html.

2. McMillan KL. Symbolic model checking. Kluwer, 1993.

3. Mateescu R, Sighireanu M. Efficient on-the-fly model-checking for regular alternation-free mu-calculus. April 2000. http://www.inrialpes.fr/vasy/ Publications/Mateescu-Sighireanu-00.html.

4. EVALUATOR Manual, 2006. http://www.inrialpes.fr/vasy/cadp/man/ evaluator.html.

5. Faci M, Logrippo L. Specifying hardware systems in LOTOS, 1993. Available at http://lotos.site.uottawa.ca/ftp/pub/Lotos/Papers/. For publication details and online versions, see Reference 9.

6. LOTOS Utilities—DILL (Digital Logic in LOTOS), July 2006. http://www.cs. stir.ac.uk/~kjt/software/lotos/dill.html.

7. Logrippo L, Faci M, Haj-Hussein M. An introduction to LOTOS. Learning by Examples, 1992.

8. Bolognesi T, Brinksma E. Introduction to the ISO Specification Language LOTOS, 1987. For publication details and online versions, see Reference 9.

9. Tutorials for CADP and LOTOS. July 2006. http://www.inrialpes.fr/vasy/cadp/ tutorial/.

## CHAPTER 5

Introducing Petri Nets

5.1 ABOUT PETRI NETS

Petri nets play an important role in the modeling, analysis, and verification of parallel systems. They are more powerful than finite state machines (automata); in particular, they provide for an efficient representation of concurrent processes. In this chapter we summarize the basic concepts concerning Petri nets. In the sequel we wish to use Petri nets as an alternative way of modeling systems and circuits.

Petri nets are a graphical as well as an algebraic modeling tool, applicable to a large variety of information processing systems. In particular, Petri nets are suitable for modeling and analyzing discrete systems, which involve a high degree of parallelism.

Most introductions to Petri nets rely on graphical representations. In this text we use both graphical as well as textual representations, making extensive use of the helpful tool PETRIFY, which will be introduced in the sequel.

5.1.1 Petri Graphs and Petri Nets

A Petri net *PN* consists of a Petri graph *PG*, together with a marking *M*. A Petri graph is a directed graph with two kinds of nodes (i.e., a "bipartite" graph), called *places* and *transitions*. Arcs are either from places to transitions or from transitions to places. In the graphical representation, places are shown as circles and transitions are shown as squares or as bars. A marking M assigns to each place p a nonnegative integer M(p). In the graphical representation, we place M(p) black dots (known as "tokens") inside the circle representing the place p. If $M(p) = k > 1$, we may also write the integer k in the circle of p.

Verification of Systems and Circuits Using LOTOS, Petri Nets, and CCS, by Michael Yoeli and Rakefet Kol
Copyright © 2008 John Wiley & Sons, Inc.

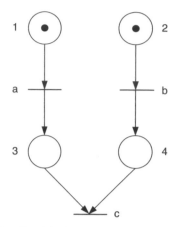

Figure 5.1   Graphical representation of Petri net X1.

Figure 5.1 shows a net X1 with four places (labeled $1, \ldots, 4$) and three transitions: a, b, c.

5.1.2   Enabling and Firing

Petri nets are intended to model dynamic systems. Places in a Petri graph correspond to system conditions, and transitions in a Petri graph correspond to system actions or events. In general, any action or event will change the system conditions. Such dynamic changes are modeled in Petri nets by their *firing* rules.

Let (p,t) be an arc in a Petri net PN, where p is a place and t is a transition. Then p is called an *input place* of t. Similarly, if (t,p) is an arc in PN, p is called an *output place* of t. A place p of PN is *marked* if $M(p) > 0$.

A transition t of PN is *enabled (firable)*, iff each input place is marked.

The *firing* of t consists in removing one token from each input place, and adding one token to each output place.

Note that a transition without any input place is always enabled.

For the time being, we consider safe nets, i.e., nets that never have more than one token in any place. In the case of such nets we may represent a marking by the set of marked places. Thus the initial marking of the net X1 from Fig. 5.1 becomes $\{1,2\}$. In the net X1 both transitions **a** and **b** are firable. If **a** fires, then the resulting marking is $\{2,3\}$. This may be written as $\{1,2\}[a > \{2,3\}$. Similarly, $\{1,2\}[b > \{1,4\}$.

Furthermore, we have the firing sequences

$$\{1,2\}[a > \{2,3\}[b > \{3,4\}[c > \{\}$$

as well as

$$\{1,2\}[b > \{1,4\}[a > \{3,4\}[c > \{\}$$

We associate with any such firing sequence its event sequence (action sequence). The event sequence belonging to the first of the above two firing sequences is $<a;b;c>$.

5.1.3 Another Definition of Petri Nets

Here is yet another set-based definition of Petri graphs and Petri nets.

A Petri graph *PG* is a triple (P, T, F), where

P is a finite set of *places*

T is a finite, nonempty set of *transitions*

F is a subset of $(P \times T) \cup (T \times P)$

Thus F is a binary relation on $(P \cup T)$, referred to as the *flow relation*.

A Petri net is a 4-tuple (P, T, F, M), where (P, T, F) is a Petri graph and M is a function from P into the set of nonnegative integers.

You can see that these definitions simply reformulate our previous definitions.

5.2 ABOUT LANGUAGES

The language of a net consists of all feasible event sequences including the empty sequence, which is denoted by λ (in the context of nets). Thus the language L(X1) of net X1 from Fig. 5.1 becomes $\{\lambda, <a>, <b>, <a;b>, <b;a>, <a;b;c>, <b;a;c>\}$. Alternatively, a shortened version to specify L(X1) is frequently used, namely

$$L(X1) = \{\lambda, a, b, ab, ba, abc, bac\}$$

We now recall some basic concepts, related to formal languages, in order to establish our terminology and our notation.

Let Σ be a finite nonempty set of symbols. Such a set is usually referred to as a finite alphabet. We refer to a finite sequence of symbols from Σ as a finite word over Σ. This also includes the empty sequence (of length 0), usually denoted by ε in connection with automata, and by λ within the theory of Petri nets. The set of all finite words over Σ is denoted by Σ^*.

If x and y are finite words, their *concatenation*, denoted by x^y, is simply the word x followed by y. For example, $<a;b>$ ^ $<c;d> = <a;b;c;d>$. If z = x^y, then x is a prefix of z. If L is the language of some Petri net, and w is a finite word in L, then evidently all prefixes of w (including λ) also belong to L. Thus L is *prefix-closed.*

Given a language L, its *prefix closure* is the smallest language L' that contains L and is prefix-closed.

5.3 ABOUT PETRIFY

PETRIFY is a powerful and efficient tool, which enables us to work with text-based representations of Petri nets. PETRIFY was developed in Barcelona, Spain under the guidance of Professor J. Cortadella.

See Reference 1 to find out more about PETRIFY, including instructions on how to get PETRIFY and its related manuals.

We now assume that you have access to PETRIFY. The following file illustrates how the net X1 described in Fig. 5.1 may be defined in PETRIFY:

File x1.net
.model x1.net
.inputs a b
.outputs c
.graph
p1 a
a p3
p2 b
b p4
p3 c
p4 c
.marking {p1 p2}
.end

We view this net as specifying a system with input events 'a' and 'b' and an output event 'c'. Hence the first four lines in the above file are self-explanatory. The next six lines represent the six arcs of the net. Note that place *j* (*j* = 1, 2, 3, 4) of net X1 is now represented by 'p*j*'. The marking shown lists the places that contain a token.

The following file represents a reduced version of file *x1.net*, as optimized by PETRIFY; Fig. 5.2 shows the graphical representation of

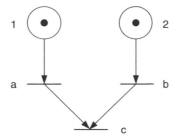

Figure 5.2   Graphical representation of Petri net X1red.

the reduced net X1red:

File x1red.net
.model x1red.net
.inputs a b
.outputs c
.graph
p1 a
p2 b
a c
b c
.marking {p1 p2}
.end

Places p3 and p4 of net X1 are "implicit places", i.e., they have exactly one incoming arc and exactly one outgoing arc. Such places may be omitted in PETRIFY descriptions. Thus lines 'a p3' and 'p3 c' may be combined into 'a c'.

You can easily convert one of the above representations of net X1 into the other by using PETRIFY as follows. The command

petrify x1.net > x1red.net

will produce the reduced net representation. From there we may restore the original version by issuing the command

petrify –ip x1red.net > x1new.net

This command will reproduce all implicit places. The outcome coincides with *x1.net*, except for a relabeling of places.

5.4 ILLUSTRATING PETRI NETS

To improve your familiarity with the preceding material, we give here some example problems together with their solutions.

Example 5.1   Let $L1 = \{\lambda,\ a,\ b,\ ab\}$. Design a Petri net E1 such that $L(E1) = L1$. Describe E1 using PETRIFY.

The following file is the required description of Petri net E1:

File E1.net
.model E1.net
.inputs a
.outputs b
.graph
p0 a
a p1
p1 a b
.marking {p0 p1}
.end

_____

Note that the line 'p1 a b' replaces the two lines 'p1 a' and 'p1 b'. The graphical representation of net E1 is given in Fig. 5.3.

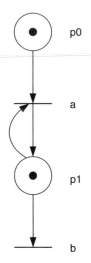

Figure 5.3   Graphical representation of Petri net E1.

You may check this solution by converting the given net E1 into a state graph E1.sg, which displays the same event sequences as net E1 (in the evident sense). This may be achieved by applying the following command (consult your manuals!):

write_sg E1.net > E1.sg

The outcome (file E1.sg) is as follows:

File E1.sg
#state graph generated by write_sg ...
#from <E1.net> ...
.model E1.net
.inputs a
.outputs b
.state graph # 4 states
s0 a s3
s0 b s1
s3 b s2
.marking {s0}
.end

Using our above method of indicating markings, states s0, s1, s2, s3 correspond to the markings {p0,p1}, {p0}, {}, {p1}, respectively.

Example 5.2   Consider the state graph *tog.sg* defined as

$$\textbf{tog.sg} = s0 \ [A > s1 \ [Y > s2 \ [A > s3 \ [Z > s0$$

This state graph represents a hardware device called a toggle, with a binary input A, and binary outputs Y and Z (as described in Section 3.3). Construct a net tog.net that is trace-equivalent to the above state graph tog.sg. That is, the two coincide with respect to their event sequences; in other words, they define the same language.

The required net is described by the following file:

File tog.net
.model tog.net
.inputs a

.outputs y z
.graph
a p0
y p1 z
z p1 y
p0 y z
p1 a
.marking {p1 <z,y>}
.end

Note that the <z,y> part of the above marking refers to a token in the corresponding implicit place.

We may check the correctness of this solution by converting this net into a state graph, using the ***write_sg*** command.

Example 5.3   Consider the language $L = \{\lambda, a, aa, aab\}$. Prove that there does not exist a Petri net PN such that $L(PN) = L$.

Let us assume that such a net PN exists, with a transition 'a' and a transition 'b'.

The transition 'b' may have four types of input places: (1) places without incoming arcs; (2) places with incoming arcs from 'a'; (3) places with incoming arcs from 'b'; (4) places with incoming arcs from 'a' and 'b'. Since 'b' is eventually firable, places of types (1) and (3) must have a token (are "marked") initially. Places of types (2) and (4) are either marked initially or become marked after the firing of 'a'. It follows that 'b' is enabled after the firing of 'a'. Hence ab is a word in L(PN), in contradiction to the above specification of L.

5.5   LABELED NETS

Labeled nets are a very useful extension of the concept of (basic, non-labeled) Petri nets that were introduced so far. In a labeled net, two or more transitions can have the same label. More formally, a *labeled net* may be defined as a triple (PN, Σ, lb), where PN = (P, T, F) is a (basic) Petri net, Σ is a finite alphabet, and lb is a function from T into ($\Sigma \cup \{\lambda\}$).

With such a labeled net we associate the language L(PN, Σ, lb), which is obtained from L(PN) by replacing each transition t, appearing in any word of L(PN), by its label lb(t).

We now indicate how labeled nets are handled in PETRIFY. To start with, consider the state graph tog.sg of Example 5.2. This state graph may be represented in PETRIFY as follows:

File tog.sg
.inputs a
.outputs y z
.state graph # 4 states
s0 a s1 y s2 a s3 z s0
.marking {s0}
.end

The entries of this file are self-explanatory.

The following command converts this state graph into a Petri net (toger.net):

petrify -er tog .sg -o toger .net

We use the -er option to get a representation that is not very concise, but is easily understood. Without the -er option we would get a concise representation, but one with a more complex structure (see the file tog.net in Section 5.4). To find out more about the -er option, consult the PETRIFY manual, as well as of Referece 2 Section 3.5.

The following is the main part of the output file toger.net:

File toger.net
.model toger.net
.inputs a
.outputs y z
.graph
a y
y a/1
z a
a/1 z
.marking { <z,a> }
.end

This is a labeled net with two transitions (denoted **a** and **a/1**), both labeled by **a**. We can also reconvert this net into a state graph using the command

write_sg toger .net -o tog .stg

The output file is as follows:

File tog.stg
.model tog.stg
.inputs a
.outputs y z
.state graph # 4 states
s1 y s2
s3 z s0
s2 a s3
s0 a s1
.marking {s0}
.end

_____

This state graph evidently coincides with the above state graph tog.sg.

EXERCISE

5.1   Now try a similar conversion, this time from a state graph to a labeled
Petri net and back, starting with tog3.sg = s0 a s1 x s2 a s3 y s4 a s5 z s0.

5.6   BOUNDED NETS

Many of the systems that we are interested in can be represented by Petri nets
that are "safe" in the following sense.

A Petri net is said to be *k-bounded*, $k > 0$, if the number of tokens in each
place does not exceed the number k for any marking reachable from the initial
marking of the net. A Petri net is said to be *safe* if it is 1-bounded.

By default, PETRIFY assumes nets to be safe.

Now consider the following net x2:

File x2.net
.model x2
.inputs a b
.outputs z
.graph
p0 a
a p1
p1 b

b p2
p2 z
.marking {p0 p2}
.end

_____

This net is evidently not safe. Namely, after 'a' and then 'b' are fired, place p2 will have two tokens. The command *petrify x2.net* will result in an error message issued, stating that a reachable marking exceeds the capacity of place p2 (assumed, by default, to be 1).

The following net x3 illustrates how such non-safe nets may be handled in PETRIFY:

File x3.net
.model x3
.inputs a b
.outputs z
.graph
p0 a
a p1
p1 b
b p2
p2 z
.capacity p2 = 3
.marking {p0 p2 = 2}
.end

_____

In this net the capacity of p2 is declared to be 3. Also, its initial marking is indicated to be 2. The command *petrify x3.net > x3s.net* converts the above net into a safe labeled net, defining the same language as x3.net. The outcome is as follows:

File x3s.net
.model x3s.net
.inputs a b
.outputs z
.graph
a b
b z/1
z z/2

z/2 z/1
p0 z
p1 a
.marking {p0 p1}
.end

EXERCISE

5.2 (a)   Convert the nets x3.net and x3s.net into state graphs and show that they are isomorphic.

   (b)   Use PETRIFY for the conversion of (a) and then prove isomorphism.

5.7   OBSERVATION EQUIVALENCE OF LPNs

We have seen how to convert a labeled Petri net LPN into a "corresponding" state graph sg(LPN). Each state of sg(LPN) represents a reachable marking of LPN. Transitions in sg(LPN) correspond to transitions in LPN, in the evident sense. In this sense, LPN and sg(LPN) are strongly equivalent. We may associate a process with sg(LPN), after replacing each λ-transition by an **i**-transition.

We will say that two LPNs, LPN1 and LPN2, are *observation-equivalent* iff this holds for the two processes associated with sg(LPN1) and sg(LPN2).

PETRIFY offers an option **-bisim** that will transform a given LPN into a reduced version, observation-equivalent to the original net LPN. But this option is not sufficient if we wish to check two LPNs for observation equivalence. The application of the above option to the two LPNs may yield two nets that are isomorphic. In such a case the two given LPNs are evidently observation-equivalent. However, this method is not general enough. If it fails, we may use CADP (see Section 4.8.2) to check the two corresponding processes for observation equivalence.

5.8   FROM BLOT TO PETRI NETS

In many cases it is quite easy to convert a Blot expression into a "corresponding" Petri net. Here "correspondence" refers to the observation equivalence between the state graph defined by the net and the LTS describing the Blot expression.

Example 5.4   Consider the Blot expression *[a;c] || *[b;c]. The correspond-
ing net is as follows:

File blot1.net

.model blot1.net
.inputs a b
.outputs c
.graph
*[a;c]
a c
c a
*[b;c]
b c
c b
.marking {<c,a> <c,b>}
.end

EXERCISES

5.3 (a)   Design the state graph corresponding to the above Blot expression.
   (b)   Confirm your design by converting the above net blot1.net into a
state graph, using PETRIFY.

5.4   Consider Exercise 2.4. Convert both sides of the equation into corresponding nets (use PETRIFY). Show that the relevant state graphs are
isomorphic, i.e., one can be obtained from the other by relabeling
the states.

5.5   Consider the following labeled net:

File ex5_5.net
.model ex5_5.net
.inputs a b
.outputs c
.graph
p0 a
a b
b a/1
a/1 b/1

b/1 c

c p0

.marking {p0}

.end

_____

(**a**) Convert this net into a trace-equivalent net where the label **b** appears only once.

(**b**) Use PETRIFY to check your solution.

5.9 LIVENESS AND PERSISTENCE

The concept of liveness is closely related to the absence of deadlocks in operating systems.

A Petri net is said to be *live* if, for any marking that has been reached from the initial marking, it is still possible to eventually fire each transition of the net by activating a suitable firing sequence.

Stated differently, if PN is a live Petri net, t is any transition of PN, and w is a word in L(PN), then there always exists a continuation of w in L(PN) terminating in t.

A Petri net is said to be *persistent* if for any two enabled transition the firing of one transition will not disable the other.

5.10 SIMPLE REDUCTION RULES

The net reduction rules (3) listed below, and illustrated in Fig. 5.4, are known to preserve the following net properties: liveness, safeness, and boundedness.

(a) **Fusion of Series Places (FSP).** Let t be a transition with a single in-place p1 and a single out-place p2. In this case, omit t and merge p1 and p2.

(b) **Fusion of Series Transitions (FST).** Let p be a place with a single in-transition t1 and a single out-transition t2. In this case, omit p and merge t1 and t2.

(c) **Fusion of Parallel Places (FPP).** Let p1 and p2 be places both having the same single in-transition and the same single out-transition. In this case, merge p1 and p2.

(d) **Fusion of Parallel Transitions (FPT)**. Similar to (c), with places and transitions interchanged.

(e) **Elimination of Self-loop Places (ESP)**. Let p be a marked place and t be a transition, where t is the single in-transition as well as the single out-transition of p. In this case, omit p.

(f) **Elimination of Self-loop Transitions (EST)**. Let t be a transition and p be a place, where p is the single in-place as well as the single out-place of t. In this case, omit t.

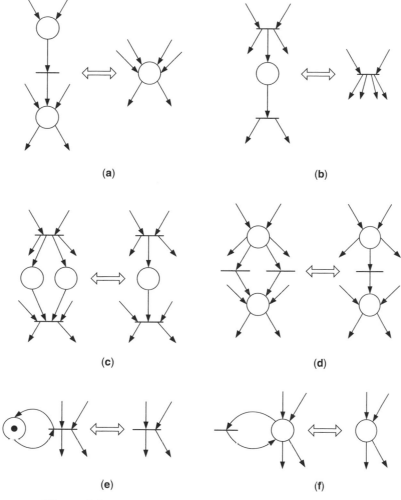

Figure 5.4 Examples of simple Petri net reduction rules.

5.11 MARKED GRAPHS

"Marked graphs" form an important subclass of Petri nets. They have been studied extensively, and their analysis is much easier than that of general Petri nets. In this section we look at some of the theory concerning marked graphs. We mainly follow the work of Commoner *et al.* (4) and Murata (3).

A *marked graph* is a Petri net having the property that every place has exactly one incoming arc and one outgoing arc.

Proposition 5.1 Every marked graph is persistent.

Proof We leave the easy proof of this proposition as an exercise.

We assume a marked graph to be represented by means of a directed graph G together with a marking M. The nodes of G represent transitions and its edges represent places. A marking M is indicated by placing tokens on the relevant arcs.

We now consider marked graphs, represented by the pair (G,M).

Let C be a simple directed circuit (cycle) of G. Thus, every node (transition) on C has exactly one incoming arc (input place) on C and exactly one outgoing arc (output place) on C. The *token count* of C in (G,M) is the sum of tokens on the arcs of C.

Proposition 5.2 Let C be a simple directed circuit in (G,M). Then the firing of any transition of (G,M) does not change the token count of C.

Proof If t is a node (transition) on C, then its firing will move one token along C, namely from its incoming arc on C to its outgoing arc on C. If t is not on C, then its firing will have no effect on C.

Proposition 5.3 A marked graph (G,M) is live iff the token count of every simple directed circuit of G is positive.

Proof If a simple directed circuit C of (G,M) is token-free, then, by Proposition 5.2, C will remain token-free after any firing sequence. Thus the nodes (transitions) on C will never be enabled.

Now assume that the token count of every simple directed circuit C of (G,M) is positive. Let v be any node of G. Consider the token-free arcs incoming to v. If there are none, then v is enabled. If not, then consider the nodes from which these arcs emanate. If they are all enabled, then v will become enabled after each one of them fires. If some are not, then consider the token-free arcs entering them, etc.

As we continue this backtracking, we are selecting a subgraph of G that consists of v, the token-free arcs entering v, the nodes from which these arcs emanate, the token-free arcs entering them, etc.

This process must terminate, since G is finite. Now, this subgraph must be circuit-free; otherwise (G,M) would contain a circuit with token count zero. Thus this subgraph must have at least one node without incoming arcs that belong to the subgraph. This node is enabled in (G,M). After firing this node, the subgraph obtained by backtracking from v over token-free arcs becomes smaller. By repeating this process, we can obtain a marking, reachable from M, in which v is enabled, be fired at least once, for any M′ reachable from M.

Thus (G,M) is live.

5.12   A SIMPLE NET ALGEBRA

In Section 5.8 we illustrated the conversion of a Blot expression into an observation-equivalent Petri net. In this section we introduce various operations on Petri nets, intended to model Blot operators. Our emphasis is on observation equivalence.

5.12.1   The Prefix Operator

As an illustrating example, consider the nets *lpn1a* and *lpn1b* represented as follows using PETRIFY:

File lpn1a.net
.model lpn1a.net
.inputs a b
.graph
p1 a
p2 b
.marking {p1 p2}
.end

File lpn1b.net
.model lpn1b.net
.inputs a b x
.graph

x a b
p0 x
.marking {x0}
.end

Note that in this example lpn1b.net = x;lpn1a.net.

Below we discuss the general case.

Let LPN = (PN,Σ,lb) be a safe labeled net, and let P(M0) be the set of places marked initially. Let x be a label not in Σ. Then we define the labeled net x;LPN as follows.

Let PN = (P,T,F,M). Assume that p0 is a place not in P. Then the set of places of x;LPN equals P ∪ {p0}.

The set of transitions of x;LPN is T ∪ {t0}, where t0 is a new transition not in T, labeled x.

Add an arc from p0 to t0. Add arcs from t0 to every place in P(M0). Put a token in p0 and remove all tokens from the places in P(M0).

We shall refer to the place p0 as the initial place of x;LPN.

The above net operator mirrors the prefix operator of Blot. Let Proc be a process strongly equivalent to the net LPN (with λ-labels replaced by **i**). Then x;Proc and x;LPN are strongly equivalent.

Consider again the net lpn1a.net defined above. This net is strongly equivalent to Proc1 = a;$ ||| b;$. The graph of reachable markings, specifying the behavior of the net lpn1a, is shown in Fig. 5.5.

The process graph of Proc1 is obtained by a relabeling of Fig. 5.5 as follows:

$$M0 \rightarrow Proc1$$

$$\{p1\} \rightarrow a;\$$$

$$\{p2\} \rightarrow b;\$$$

$$\{\} \rightarrow \$$$

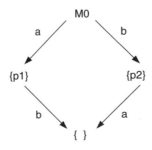

Figure 5.5   Graphical representation of Petri net lpn1a.

We now extend the process graph of Proc1 to that of x;Proc1 and the above net lpn1a to the above net lpn1b = x;lpn1a.

The corresponding two graphs are again isomorphic, and consequently, x;Proc1 and x;lpn1a are strongly equivalent.

EXERCISE

5.6 Use CADP and PETRIFY to confirm that x;lpn1a and x;Proc1 are strongly equivalent.

5.12.2 The Choice Operator

The net choice operator is intended to mirror the choice operator of Blot. Let x1;LPN1, . . . , xk;LPNk be safe, labeled Petri nets. Assume that they have been constructed as explained in the preceding section. We define their *choice* x1;LPN1 [ ] . . . [ ] xk;LPNk as the net obtained by merging all the initial places of the k nets into a single marked place p0.

One easily verifies that this construct indeed mirrors the choice operator of Blot.

EXERCISE

5.7 Let Proc2 = *[a;b] [ ] *[b;c]. Use the above method to construct a labeled Petri net observation-equivalent to Proc2. Use CADP and PETRIFY to verify your construction.

5.12.3 The Star Operator

Before defining the star operator for nets, we introduce the concept of Δ-net. Such a net is a safe labeled net with a unique start node (a node without incoming arcs), which is a marked place. All other places are not marked. Furthermore, all terminal nodes (i.e., nodes without outgoing arcs) are transitions.

Given a Δ-net LPN1, its star closure *LPN1 is obtained by connecting each terminal transition to the start place of LPN1. Recall now our use of *Proc. Namely, if Proc = **seq**, where **seq** is a finite nonempty sequence of events, P = ***seq** is defined by P = **seq**;P. Furthermore, P = *[**seq1** [ ] . . . [ ] **seqk**] is defined by P = **seq1**;P [ ] . . . [ ] **seqk**;P. Assume now that *Proc1 is defined and that Proc1 and LPN1 are strongly equivalent. Then so are *LPN1 and *Proc1. In the following section we illustrate such an equivalence of *-expressions by an example.

Example 5.5 In Section 3.2.4 we introduced the 2-input XOR-gate. Below we represent this module by using Blot, and by using our Petri net algebra, to illustrate the connection between the two representations.

Let XOR.net = *(a;z;{} [ ] b;z;{}). Similarly, let XOR.lot be defined by the Blot expression XOR.lot = *[a;z [ ] b;z]. It is quite easy to prove that XOR.net and XOR.lot are strongly equivalent, using PETRIFY and CADP. To achieve this goal, we may proceed as follows. First, we convert the above specification of XOR.net into the corresponding PETRIFY description as follows:

File xor.net
.model xor.net
.inputs a b
.outputs z
.graph
p0 a
a z
p0 b
b z/1
so far we have specified the net (a;z;{} [ ] b;z;{})
next we provide recursion
z p0
z/1 p0
.marking {p0}
.end

_____

Next, we convert XOR.lot into the corresponding LOTOS program:

File xor.lotos
specification xor[a,b,z]: noexit behaviour
      xor[a,b,z]
where
  process xor[a,b,z]:noexit:=
      a;z;xor[a,b,z] [] b;z;xor[a,b,z]
  endproc
endspec

_____

To prove that **xor.net** and **xor.lotos** are strongly equivalent, we convert both into their state graphs, which turn out to be strongly equivalent.

5.12.4   Parallel Compositions

Next we discuss parallel compositions of labeled nets and relate such compositions to the concepts of parallel compositions defined in Blot.

5.12.4.1   The Basic Approach   Consider two labeled nets, LPN1 and LPN2, and assume that the label b (other than λ) appears only once in each net. Then LPN1|[b]|LPN2 is defined as the net obtained from LPN1 and LPN2 by merging into a single transition the two original transitions labeled b. This merged transition is again labeled b. To illustrate, let net X1 = a;b;c;{} and net X2 = d;b;{}. Their composition X1|[b]|X2 is shown in Fig. 5.6.

It is easy to verify that the net X1|[b]|X2 and the Blot expression a;b;c;$|[b]|d;b;$ are strongly equivalent.

5.12.4.2   The Multiple-Labeled Case   To handle this general case, we first need to define the concept of *transition splitting*.

Let *t* be a transition of a labeled net. By *splitting transition t* into *k* parts we refer to the replacement of *t* by *k* new transitions. The input and output places of the new transitions are the same as those of the replaced transition *t*.

The following technique of constructing the parallel composition of two labeled nets is based on the work of Reference 5.

Let LPN1 and LPN2 be labeled nets with *m* and *n* appearances of the label b, respectively. The following procedure describes how to generate the parallel composition LPN1|[b]|LPN2. To simplify our notation, let *m* = 2 and *n* = 3.

(1) Relabel the two b-labels of net LPN1 as b/1 and b/2.
(2) Relabel the three b-labels of net LPN2 as b/1, b/2, b/3.

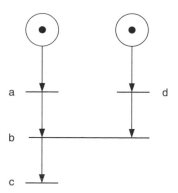

Figure 5.6   Graphical representation of parallel composition X1|[b]|X2.

(3) Split each transition labeled b/i $(i = 1, 2)$ of LPN1 into three new transitions, labeled $b/i/1$, $b/i/2$, $b/i/3$.

(4) Split each transition labeled b/j $(j = 1, 2, 3)$ of LPN2 into two new transitions, labeled $b/1/j$ and $b/2/j$.

(5) Merge each pair of equally labeled transitions of LPN1 and LPN2.

(6) Relabel each merged pair obtained by (5) as b.

Assume that LPNk and Proc$k$ $(k = 1, 2)$ are strongly equivalent. It can be shown that LPN1|[b]|LPN2 and Proc1|[b]|Proc2 are strongly equivalent. For a detailed proof, see Reference 5.

The above net composing procedure is easily extended to the case of LPN1 $|[b_1, \ldots, b_h]|$ LPN2.

EXERCISE

5.8   Let $\mathbf{P}$ = *[a;b] and $\mathbf{Q}$ = *[c;a;d;a]. Use CADP as well as PETRIFY to represent $\mathbf{P} \| \mathbf{Q}$. Then generate and compare the corresponding state graphs.

5.13   ARC-WEIGHTED NETS

We now introduce the concept of "arc-weighted nets", as an extension of the concept of Petri net, as defined in Section 5.1.

An *arc-weighted net* is a 5-tuple (P, T, F, W, M), where (P, T, F, M) is a Petri net and W, the *weight function*, is a mapping from $(P \times T) \cup (T \times P)$ into $\{1, 2, 3, \ldots\}$.

5.13.1   Enabling and Firing in Arc-Weighted Nets

Let PN $= (P, T, F, W, M)$ be an arc-weighted net. Let t be a transition of PN, i.e., an element of T. The transition t is *enabled* in PN if each input place p of t (see Section 5.1) is marked with at least $W(p, t)$ tokens.

If t is enabled, then its firing removes $W(p, t)$ tokens from each input place of t and adds $W(t, q)$ tokens to each output place q of t.

Example 5.6   Let arc.net be the net (P, T, F, W, M) shown in Fig. 5.7. Let $M(p0) = 2$, $M(p1) = 0$. Then the transition a is enabled, and its firing results in the marking M', where $M'(p0) = 1$, $M'(p1) = 1$. Note that the marking M' enables only transition a (for a second time), but not

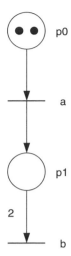

Figure 5.7 Graphical representation of Petri net arc.net.

transition b. Only after transition a fires for a second time will transition b
be enabled.

In the PETRIFY representation of an arc-weighted net, the entry

$$p1 \; b \; (2)$$

indicates that the arc from place p1 to transition b has weight 2.

Thus the net arc.net of Fig. 5.7 has the following PETRIFY representation:

File arc.net
.model arc.net
.inputs a
.outputs b
.graph
p0 a
a p1
p1 b (2)
capacity p0 = 3 p1 = 3
.marking {p0 = 2}
.end

We may simplify the above file by issuing the command *petrify arc.net -o
arc1.net*.

The outcome is the non-weighted, labeled net arc1.net, the main part of which is as follows:

Part of File arc1.net
.graph
p0 a
a a/1
a/1 b
.marking {p0}
.end

_____

We may also issue the command ***write_sg arc.net -o arc.sg***. The outcome is the state-graph

$$s0[a > s1[a > s2[b > s3.$$

5.13.2   Arc-Weighted Versus Non-Labeled Nets

The question arises, whether for any given arc-weighted net we may construct a non-weighted, non-labeled net that defines the same language. The answer is negative, as illustrated by the net arc.net, specified above. The non-existence of a language-equivalent non-weighted, non-labeled net follows immediately from Example 5.3 above.

EXERCISE

5.9   Consider the following arc-weighted net:

File arcx.net
.model arcx.net
.inputs a b c
.outputs d
.graph
p1 a
p2 b
p3 c
a p0
b p0
c p0
p0 d (2)

.capacity p0 = 3
.marking {p1 p2 p3}
.end

_____

(a) Construct the corresponding state graph.

(b) Use PETRIFY to confirm your construction.

5.14 READERS–WRITERS SYSTEM

We now illustrate the application of arc-weighted nets to the representation of a readers–writers system. In such a system up to k ($k > 1$) processes may be reading concurrently from a shared memory, but only one process may be writing into the shared memory. Furthermore, writing is possible only if no other process is reading at the same time.

5.14.1 A Readers–Writers System Net Representation

Figure 5.8 (based on of Reference 3 Figure 11) shows an arc-weighted net representing such a system. The four transitions represent the following events:

rin	a process starts reading
rout	a process ends reading
win	a process starts writing
wout	a process ends writing

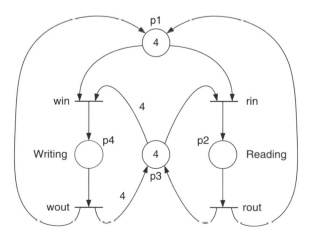

Figure 5.8 Graphical representation of Petri net rw.net.

The number of tokens in place p2 indicates the number of presently reading processes. A token in place p4 indicates that a process is presently writing. Using PETRIFY, the net of Fig. 5.8 is as follows (assuming $k = 4$):

File rw.net
.model rw.net
.inputs rin win rout wout
.graph
p1 rin
p1 win
rin p2
win p4
p2 rout
p4 wout
p3 rin
p3 win (4)
rout p1 p3
wout p1
wout p3 (4)
.capacity p1 = 4 p3 = 4 p2 = 4
.marking {p1 = 4 p3 = 4}
.end

_____

5.14.2 Verification of a Readers–Writers System

We wish to prove that the net of Fig. 5.8 satisfies the following requirements:

[**RW1**]   Only one process can be writing at any time, and in this case no process may be reading.
[**RW2**]   From 1 to k processes may be reading concurrently, provided no process is writing.

To confirm the above two requirements, we observe that $M(p2) + M(p3) + k \times M(p4) = k$.

It is easy to verify that this equation also applies to any marking M' reachable from M. It follows that $M'(p4) < 2$, and that $M'(p4) = 1$ implies $M'(p2) = M'(p3) = 0$; that is, [RW1] is satisfied. Furthermore, $M'(p2)$ may assume any value between 1 and k, provided that $M'(p4) = 0$. Thus [RW2] is also satisfied.

5.15 INHIBITOR NETS

5.15.1 Introduction to Inhibitor Nets

Inhibitor nets provide an important extension of the concept of Petri nets. They are formed by the addition of *inhibitor arcs* to the type of labeled nets defined in Section 5.5. If a net contains an inhibitor arc from place p to transition t, this transition may not fire, as long as place p contains one or more tokens. In the graphical representation of an inhibitor net, an inhibitor arc from place p to transition t terminates in a small circle ("bubble") at the transition t, rather than the usual arrow symbol. In the PETRIFY representation such an inhibitor arc is indicated by

$$p \ t \ (0)$$

Example 5.7   The following is the PETRIFY representation of an example of an inhibitor net inh1.net, whose graphical representation is shown in Fig. 5.9:

File inh1.net
.model inh1.net
.inputs a
.outputs b c
.graph
p0 a
a p1
p1 b
p1 c (0)
.capacity p0 = 2 p1 = 2
.marking {p0 = 2}
.end

————————

EXERCISE

5.10(a)   Construct a state graph, language-equivalent with inh1.net.

   (b)   Use PETRIFY to confirm (a).

5.15.2 The Expressive Power of Inhibitor Nets

Inhibitor nets can be constructed that are "more powerful" than labeled nets without inhibitor arcs, i.e., there does not exist a language-equivalent

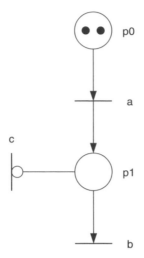

Figure 5.9   Graphical representation of inhibitor net inh1.net.

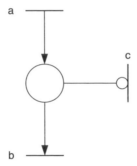

Figure 5.10   Inhibitor net inh2.net.

labeled net. For a proof of this statement, see Reference 6. Such an inhibitor net inh2.net is shown in Fig. 5.10.

5.16   TRUE CONCURRENCY

In the specification and description of asynchronous designs it is customary to replace true concurrency (i.e., two or more events happening simultaneously) by "non-deterministic interleaving" (i.e., the events in question happen one after the other, in any order). This is usually done for the sake of simplicity, without investigating the loss of information caused by such a replacement. In this section we show how Petri nets may be used to distinguish between the true concurrency model and the interleaving model. We also refer to studies indicating under which conditions such a replacement is justified.

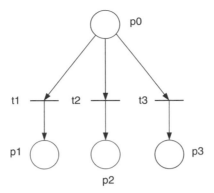

Figure 5.11 Net PN5.11.

5.16.1 The Pi-Language

Definition 5.1 Let PN = (P, T, F, M) be a Petri net, as defined in Section 5.1. Let U be a non-empty subset of T. U is *concurrently firable* in PN iff the marking M(p) of every place p is not less than the number of arcs from p to transitions in U. If this is the case, then we write M[U>, assuming PN to be given.

As an example, consider the net of Fig. 5.11. Here, if M(p0) = 3, all three transitions are concurrently firable. If M(p0) = 2, any two of the three transitions are concurrently firable.

Definition 5.2 Let M[U> in PN be as defined in Definition 5.1. The outcome M' of firing U concurrently is the marking obtained by firing each transition in U, in any order, and we write M[U > M'. It is easy to verify that M' does not depend on the order in which the transitions of U are fired.

In the example of Fig. 5.11, let M(p0) = 3, U = {t1,t2}, and M[U > M'. Then M'(p0) = M'(p1) = M'(p2) = 1, and M'(p3) = 0.

Definition 5.3 Let PN be as above, and let M1, M2, ... be reachable markings. Let M = M0[U1 > M1, M1[U2 > M2, ..., M(k − 1)[Uk > Mk. We say that U1, U2, ..., Uk is a *multiple-firing sequence* of PN, and denote by pi(PN) = π(PN) the set of all feasible multiple-firing sequences of PN, including the empty sequence Λ.

For more information about the Pi-language, refer to Reference 7.

5.16.2 Pi-Equivalence

The above considerations are easily extended to labeled nets. We leave the details to our readers (cf. Reference 7).

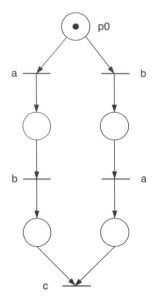

Figure 5.12   Labeled net LPN5.12.

Let LPN1 and LPN2 be labeled nets. We say that they are *pi-equivalent* iff pi(LPN1) = pi(LPN2).

Let L(LPN) denote the language of the labeled net LPN, as defined in Section 5.5. If L(LPN1) = L(LPN2), then the two nets are *L-equivalent*.

In general, L-equivalence does not imply pi-equivalence. For example, compare the net LPN5.12 shown in Fig. 5.12 with that of Fig. 5.1. The two nets are evidently L-equivalent, but are not pi-equivalent. Only the net of Fig. 5.1 admits the multiple-firing sequence $<\{a,b\},\{c\}>$!

5.16.3   Concurrency-Preserving Synthesis

The distinction between L-equivalence and pi-equivalence is important in connection with *concurrency-preserving synthesis* approaches. Indeed, most of the decomposition and synthesis approaches discussed so far are concurrency-preserving. To be more precise, we introduce the following notation.

Let **a&b** denote the set $\{$**a;b, b;a,** $\{$**a,b**$\}\}$. We define **a&b&c** similarly.

For example, $\{$**a,b,c**$\}$ and (**a&c);b** are elements of **a&b&c**.

Consider now the two nets CEL3spec.net and CEL3impl.net, shown in Fig. 5.13. CEL3impl.net is a type-D realization (see Section 7.7) of CEL3spec.net. We want to show that this realization is concurrency-preserving. For this purpose, we look at pi(CEL3spec.net) = *[(**a&b&c);z**]. This expression forms part of pi(CEL3impl.net), after the internal variable y is omitted. This shows that the degree of concurrency specified is preserved in its implementation.

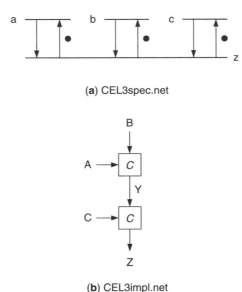

(**a**) CEL3spec.net

(**b**) CEL3impl.net

Figure 5.13 CEL3spec and CEL3impl nets.

5.17 FURTHER READING

We recommend that you get a glimpse at the "world of Petri nets" (8). Follow the "Introductions" link there, and in particular, have a look at the introductory paper of Murata (3), as well as at the "Lectures on Petri Nets I" (9).

For another approach to a rather simple net algebra, see Reference 10.

For additional material dealing with reader–writer systems, see pages 66–69 of Reference 11 and page 546 of Reference 3. For more information on inhibitor nets, see Reference 6. For further insight into the topic of true concurrency, we recommend References 7, 12, 13, and 14.

5.18 SELECTED SOLUTIONS

5.2(b) Just apply the command *write_sg* to both x3.net and x3s.net. Show that the outcomes differ only in their state labeling.

5.3(b) Apply *write_sg* to blot1.net. You will get the following state graph:

File blot1.sg

s0 a s2

s0 b s1

s2 b s3

s1 a s3

s3 c s0

.marking {s0}

_____

5.4 The construction of the net representing the left-hand side of the equation is straightforward. The net representing the right-hand side is as follows; applying PETRIFY to this representation shows that both nets are strongly equivalent:

File ex5_4b.net

.model ex5_4b.net

.inputs a

.outputs b c

.graph

p0 a

a b

b c

c p0

p0 b/1

b/1 a/1

a/1 c/1

c/1 p0

.marking {p0}

.end

_____

5.5 (a) The required net is as follows:

File ex5_5a.net

.model ex5_5a.net

.inputs a b c

.graph

a p1 c

b p0

c a/1

a/1 p1 a

p0 a c

p1 b
.marking $\{<c,a/1>\}$
.end

———————

(b) Apply the command

> *write_sg ex5_5a.net*

You will get a state graph trace-equivalent to the net ex5_5.net.

5.6 The corresponding LOTOS and PETRIFY files are as follows:

File ex5_6.lotos
specification ex5_6[a,b,x]:exit behaviour
    x;(a;exit ||| b;exit)
endspec

———————

File ex5_6.net
.inputs x
.outputs a b
.graph
p0 x
x a b
.marking {p0}
.end

———————

Now derive the relevant state graphs and confirm that they are isomorphic.

5.7 The corresponding LOTOS and PETRIFY files are as follows:

File ex5_7.lotos
specification ex5_7[a,b,c]:noexit behaviour
      cy2[a,b] [] cy2[b,c]

where
  process cy2[a,b]:noexit: =
    a;b;cy2[a,b]
  endproc
endspec

File ex5_7.net
.inputs a b c
.graph
p0 a b
a p1
p1 b/1
b/1 a/1
a/1 p1
b p2
p2 c
c b/2
b/2 p2
.marking {p0}
.end

Now proceed as in Exercise 5.6.

5.8 The relevant PETRIFY file is as follows; note that we applied
transition-splitting to the transition **a** of **P**:

File ex5_8.net
.inputs a b c d
.graph
#process P
p0 a a/1
a p1
a/1 p1
p1 b
b p0

```
#process Q
p2 c
c a
a d
d a/1
a/1 p2
.marking {p0 p2}
.end
```

The corresponding LOTOS file ex5_8.lotos is designed similarly to Exercise 5.7. From the above file ex5_8.net derive the corresponding state graph. Then transform the file ex5_8.lotos into the corresponding omin-file. The two state graphs are again isomorphic.

5.9(b)   Use the command

   write_sg arcx.net -o arcx.sg

to get the required state graph.

5.10(b)   Use again the corresponding command ***write_sg***, as above.

5.19 REFERENCES

1. PETRIFY: a tool for synthesis of Petri nets and asynchronous circuits. UPC-DAC VLSI CAD Group, 1999. http://www.lsi.upc.es/petrify/.
2. Cortadella J, Kishinevsky M, Kondratyev A, Lavagno L, Yakovlev A. Logic synthesis for asynchronous controllers and interfaces. Springer, 2002.
3. Murata T. Petri nets: properties, analysis and applications. Proc IEEE, 1989;77(4):541–580.
4. Commoner F, Holt AW, Even S, Pnueli A. Marked directed graphs. J Comput Syst Sci 1971;5(5):511–523.
5. Reicher I, Yoeli M. Net-based modeling and verification of asynchronous circuits. TR 463, Computer Science Department, Technion, Haifa, 1987.
6. Porat S, Yoeli M. Towards a hierarchy of nets. J Comput Syst Sci 1984;29(2):198–206.
7. Yoeli M, Etzion T. Behavioral equivalence of concurrent systems. In: Applications and theory of Petri nets. Informatik-Fachberichte 66. Springer, 1983.

8. Petri Nets World Online Services for the International Petri Nets Community, 2007. http://www.informatik.uni-hamburg.de/TGI/PetriNets/.

9. Reisig W, Rozenberg G, editors. Lectures on Petri nets I: Basic models, advances in Petri nets. Lecture Notes in Computer Science, Vol. 1491. Springer, 1998.

10. de Jong GG, Lin B. A communicating Petri net model for the design of concurrent asynchronous modules. ACM/IEEE DAC 1994:49–55. http://portal.acm.org/citation.cfm?id=196272.

11. Peterson JL. Petri net theory and the modeling of systems. Prentice-Hall, 1981.

12. Rozenberg G, Verraedt R. Subset languages of Petri nets I: the relationship to string languages and normal forms. Theor Comp Sci 1983;26:301–326.

13. Silver SJ, Brzozowski JA. True concurrency in models of asynchronous circuit behavior. Formal Meth Syst Design 2003;22(3):183–203.

14. Yen H-C. Sequential versus concurrent languages of labeled conflict-free Petri nets. IEEE Trans Autom Control 2002;47(7):1158–1162.

## CHAPTER 6

Introducing CCS

6.1 ABOUT CCS

CCS (Calculus of Communication Systems) is a theory of communicating systems, developed by Robin Milner (1, 2). Note that LOTOS (see Chapter 4) is based on CCS, as well as on Hoare's CSP (3). This chapter provides an introduction to the theory of CCS, and to its related tool CWB-NC. In the following chapters we describe a variety of applications of CCS. For a recommendable tutorial on CCS and its applications, see Reference (4).

6.2 OPERATORS 'PREFIX' AND 'SUM'

The CCS concept of *agent* corresponds to that of process introduced in Chapter 2.

The CCS prefix operator, denoted by '.', plays the same role as the LOTOS (or Blot) prefix operator ';'. Furthermore, the CCS sum operator '+' corresponds to the LOTOS/Blot choice operator '[]'. For example, let **VM2** be the vending machine specified in Blot in Chapter 2. Recall that this vending machine operates only once. We repeat its Blot specification:

$$\text{VM2} := \text{coin;(coffee;\$ [] tea;\$)}$$

The corresponding agent is specified in CCS as follows:

$$\text{VM2\_ccs} := \text{coin.(coffee.nil + tea.nil)}$$

Note that the trivial process that does nothing, and is denoted by '$\$$' in Blot, is denoted by '**nil**' (also '**0**') in CCS. In Chapter 2 we introduced process graphs as a way to represent processes. In CCS such process

Verification of Systems and Circuits Using LOTOS, Petri Nets, and CCS, by
Michael Yoeli and Rakefet Kol
Copyright © 2008 John Wiley & Sons, Inc.

graphs are known as "transition diagrams" (see Reference 4). The process graph representing **VM2**, as defined above, was shown in Fig. 2.3.

In view of the above correspondence between CCS and Blot, the process graph of Fig. 2.3 may be converted into an isomorphic transition diagram, representing **VM2.ccs**, by the following renaming of node labels:

$$
\begin{array}{ll}
\text{VM2.blot} & \rightarrow \text{VM2.ccs} \\
\text{coffee;\$ [] tea;\$} & \rightarrow \text{coffee.nil + tea.nil} \\
\$ & \rightarrow \text{nil}
\end{array}
$$

The outcome is the transition diagram shown in Fig. 6.1.

6.2.1 Semantics

The semantics of CCS is defined by a set of rules enabling us to convert a CCS expression into a transition diagram as well as into an LTS (see Chapter 2).

The rules for the prefix and sum operators are as follows (cf. Reference 4):

Rule 6.1:   **a.P [a > P**
Rule 6.2(a):   If **P[a > P'**, then **P + Q [a > P'**
Rule 6.2(b):   If **Q[a > Q'**, then **P + Q [a > Q'**

In the above rules 'a' denotes an arbitrary event, and capital letters (**P**, etc.) represent agents. Recall that the meaning of **P[a > P'** is "the event 'a' is applicable to **P** and the relevant outcome is **P'**."

You can verify that the application of the above rules to the above agent expression defining VM2_ccs will directly yield the transition diagram shown in Fig. 6.1.

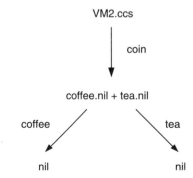

Figure 6.1   VM2.ccs transition diagram.

6.3 RECURSION

Consider the concept of "recursive definition", introduced in Chapter 2. Recursive agents may similarly be specified in CCS. For example, recall the specification of VM3 in Chapter 2. When replacing ';' by '.', '[]' by '+', and '=' by ':=', we get

VM3_ccs := in2p.big.collect.VM3_ccs+in1p.little.collect.VM3_ccs

This is actually the way this vending machine was represented originally in Reference 2.

6.3.1 Semantics

The following rule applies to the above definition symbol ':=':

Rule 6.3:   If **A := P** and **P[a > P'**, then **A[a > P'**

It follows, for example, that

VM3_ccs[in2p > big.collect.VM3_ccs

As indicated above, process graphs, introduced in Chapter 2, are referred to as transition diagrams in CCS. Figure 6.2 shows the transition diagram for the above agent **VM3_ccs**.

6.4 CONCURRENCY OPERATOR

The way in which concurrency is handled in CCS differs considerably from the approach valid in Blot (presented in Chapter 2) and LOTOS (presented in Chapter 4).

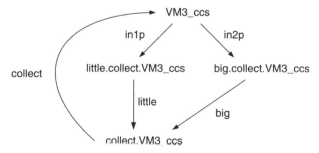

Figure 6.2   VM3_ccs transition diagram.

To start, consider the two agents **A1:= a.b.nil** and **A2:= a.c.nil**. Assume that **a** in **A2** is an output, connected to an input **a** in **A1**. In CCS we distinguish between the two **a**'s by a suitable notation. Namely, we use '**a** to denote **a** in the role of an output. This notation is taken over from the CCS-oriented tool CWB (Concurrency Work bench), which is presented in Section 6.8. In a more familiar notation, **a**(overlined) is used instead of '**a**.

We now amend **A2** by replacing **a** by '**a**. Thus **A2** is now defined as '**a.c.nil**.

The CCS concurrency operator is '**|**'. In general, given two CCS expressions **P** and **Q**, the composite process **P | Q** is given by the following three rules:

Rule 6.4(a):   If **P[a > P'**, then **P | Q [a > P' | Q**

This rule implies that if **P** is an agent that can perform action **a** and become **P'**, then **P | Q** can perform action **a**, and become **P' | Q**.

The following rule is the symmetrical rule for **Q**:

Rule 6.4(b):   If **Q[a > Q'**, then **P | Q [a > P | Q'**

Rule 6.4(c):   If **P[c > P'** and **Q['c > Q'**, then **P | Q [τ> P' | Q'** where τ denotes an internal action not observable from the outside

Applying these rules to the above example, we obtain:

(a) **A1 | A2 [a> b.nil | A2**

(b) **A1 | A2 ['a> A1 | c.nil**

(c) **A1 | A2 [τ> b.nil | c.nil**

6.5 EQUIVALENCES

In Chapter 2 we defined strong equivalence between processes, as well as observation equivalence. Both definitions also apply to CCS agents (with '**i**' replaced by 'τ'). In Section 6.8.2 we show how such equivalences may be checked, using the CWB tool.

6.6 RESTRICTION

Given a CCS expression, we may "restrict" one or more events, using the *restriction operator* '****'. For example, the CCS expressions **a.b.c.nil\{b}** and **a.nil** are strongly equivalent. The relevant rule is as follows:

Rule 6.5:   If **P[a > P'**, then **P\L [a > P'\L**, provided neither **a** nor '**a** is in **L**

6.7 CTL

In Section 6.8 we introduce the Concurrency Workbench CWB-NC, and show how this powerful tool may be used to check CCS-specified systems with respect to equivalences, as well as a variety of properties. One way of formulating such properties is offered by CTL (Computation Tree Logic). For a detailed exposition of CTL, we recommend the work of Clarke *et al.* (5). Here we present a short summary of CTL.

6.7.1 Introducing CTL

CTL is usually defined with respect to a labeled, directed graph, called a "Kripke structure". Such a structure is a triple $M = (S, R, L)$, where S is a finite set of states and R is a binary relation on S. sRt means that state t is an immediate successor of state s. We assume that every state in S has at least one immediate successor. L is a "labeling" function, associating with each state a subset of a given fixed set of "atomic" propositions. Properties of such structures are defined by means of "temporal operators".

In CTL temporal operators occur in pairs consisting of A (for All) or E (for Exists), followed by F (for Finally true), G (for Globally true), X (for neXt), U (for strong Until), or W (for Weak until).

The syntax of CTL formulas may be described as follows:

- Every atomic proposition is a CTL formula.
- If f and g are CTL formulas, then so are $\sim$f, $(f \wedge g)$, AXf, EXf, A(fUg), E(fUg), A(fWg)

The other operators may be derived from those listed above as follows:

$$f \vee g = \sim(\sim f \wedge \sim g)$$

$$AFf = A(\text{true } U \text{ f})$$

$$EFf = E(\text{true } U f)$$

$$AGf = \sim E(\text{true } U \sim f)$$

$$EGf = A(\text{true } U \sim f)$$

Informally, for example, AXf means "every next state satisfies f", EXf means "there exists a next state that satisfies f", and AGf means "every reachable state satisfies f".

The semantics of all the above formulas is formally explained below.

A path of a model $M = (S, R, L)$ is an infinite sequence (s.0, s.1,), such that s.$i + 1$ is an immediate successor of s.i.

Let $M = (S, R, L)$ be given, and let s be a state of M. We write $s \vDash f$ to state that f is true in state s. The following rules apply:

$s \vDash p$ iff $p \in L(s)$, where p is an atomic proposition

$s.0 \vDash AXf$ iff for every path $(s.0, s.1, \dots)$ $s.1 \vDash f$

$s.0 \vDash EXf$ iff for some path $(s.0, s.1, \dots)$ $s.1 \vDash f$

$s.0 \vDash A(f \ U \ g)$ iff for all paths $(s.0, s.1, \dots)$, for some i,

$\quad s.i \vDash g$ and for all $j < i$, $s.j \vDash f$

$s.0 \vDash E(f \ U \ g)$ iff for some path $(s.0, s.1, \dots)$, for some i,

$\quad s.i \vDash g$ and for all $j < i$, $s.j \vDash f$

Thus A means "for every path", and E means "for some path". F means "eventually" (i.e., for some $s.i$), G means "always" (i.e., for every $s.i$). The logical connectives have their usual meaning.

In Section 6.8.8 we illustrate the application and use of CTL to the verification of CCS-based systems, using CWB-NC.

6.8   THE CONCURRENCY WORKBENCH (CWB)

At this point we recommend that you obtain and use the Concurrency Workbench (CWB) to become better acquainted with the preceding rules, as well as to learn more about the ways of analyzing CCS agents. Various versions of the CWB are presently available. Here we introduce the CWB-NC version. "NC" stood originally for "North Carolina", where this version was developed. However, the team involved moved some time later to SUNY at Stony Brook, and renamed their version "Concurrency Workbench of the New Century". This version is freely available; for details, go to Reference 6. The site provides a lot of educational material. It also contains an extensive manual, parts of which will form the basis of the following material. It is noteworthy that CWB-NC also provides some assistance for analyzing Basic LOTOS programs.

6.8.1   The 'sim' and 'compile' Commands

To obtain an illustration of the application of some of the rules listed above, install and familiarize yourself with CWB-NC. Select the ccs-option and, upon receiving the CWB-NC prompt (**cwb-nc**>), issue, for example, the command

$$\textbf{sim ``a.b.nil + c.nil''}$$

You will then be given the corresponding derivation tree, shown here in a more concise format:

a.b.nil + c.nil
1: [c> nil
2: [a> b.nil [b> nil

_____

Next, try

$$\textbf{sim ``a.nil | b.nil''}$$

You will get

a.nil | b.nil
1: [a> nil| b.nil [b> nil|nil
2: [b> a.nil |nil [a> nil|nil

_____

Now try

$$\textbf{sim `` `a.b.nil | a.c.nil''}$$

The initial outcome will be

1: [t> b.nil | c.nil
2: [a> `a.b.nil | c.nil
3: [`a> b.nil | a.c.nil

_____

Note that 't' replaces the Greek letter 'τ'.

The '**compile**' command provides the facility to construct a labeled transition system (LTS) corresponding to a given CCS agent, in accordance with the semantic rules introduced in the preceding sections.

To illustrate this, issue the following command at the CWB prompt (**cwb-nc**>):

$$\textbf{compile b.nil + c.t.nil}$$

The outcome is the following LTS:

(0,b,1)
(0,c,2)
(2,t,1)
Start States [0]

_____

The above two commands are also applicable to agents that are defined recursively. To illustrate, enter the following file into, say, your local C: directory:

File cycle1.ccs
proc cycle1 = a.b.cycle1

_____

Now go to CWB-NC, and issue the command

load C:\cycle1.ccs

followed by

compile cycle1

You will get a version of the relevant LTS:
(0,a,1)
(1,b,0)

_____

Try also the command

sim "cycle1".

You will get another version of the above LTS.

6.8.2   Checking Equivalences

We now wish to use CWB-NC to check equivalences. Assume, for example, that we wish to know whether "**b.nil + c.t.nil**" and "**c.nil + b.nil**" are observation-equivalent. This may be achieved by using the command

eq "b.nil+c.t.nil" "c.nil+b.nil"

You will get 'TRUE'.

The **eq** command is also applicable to agents defined recursively. We assume that the file **cycle1.ccs** is still loaded into your CWB-NC system. To verify, for example, that **a.b.cycle1** and **a.b.a.b.cycle1** are strongly equivalent, issue the command

eq -S bisim a.b.cycle1 a.b.a.b.cycle1

You will obtain 'TRUE'.

CWB-NC may also be used to check trace equivalence. Recall that two processes are trace-equivalent, if they define the same language. To check trace equivalence, we issue the command

eq -S trace agent1 agent2

Alternatively, we may apply the command

eq -Smay agent1 agent2

To illustrate this, issue the command

eq -Smay a.b.nil+a.c.nil a.(b.nil+c.nil)

You will obtain 'TRUE'.

However, if you omit the '**-Smay**' part, you will obtain FALSE.

Indeed, as you are in no doubt aware by now, the two agents are not observation-equivalent. In Section 6.8.5 we show how to obtain counterexamples if the two agents are not equivalent.

Note that we may also check language inclusion. The relevant command is

le -Smay agent1 agent2

This command will check whether L(agent1) is a subset of L(agent2).

6.8.3   Checking Restrictions

The following command gives an example of the use of the restriction operator:

eq -S bisim a.nil a.b.c.nil\\{b}

The outcome is 'TRUE'.

6.8.4   HML Formulas

If two agents are not equivalent, we may use CWB-NC to obtain counterexamples. Such counterexamples are represented by means of "Hennessy–Milner Logic (HML)" formulas. Such formulas are defined as follows.

Let T be an LTS (Labeled Transition System—see Chapter 2). We define inductively, when a state s of T satisfies the HML formula φ (notation: $s \vDash \varphi$):

$s \vDash tt$ holds for every state s of T (here 'tt' stands for TRUE)
not ($s \vDash ff$) again holds for every state s of T ('ff' stands for FALSE)
$s \vDash [a]\varphi$ iff for all t with s[a>t, $t \vDash \varphi$
$s \vDash <a>\varphi$ iff for some t with s[a>t, $t \vDash \varphi$
the logical connectives $\wedge$ and $\vee$ have their usual meaning

We may use the '**chk**' command to find out whether a given agent satisfies a given HML formula. Here are some examples:

chk a.b.nil+a.c.nil <a> [b]tt

Outcome: TRUE

Note that the '**chk**' command refers to the initial state of the given agent. Thus the above HML formula states that there exists an **a**-transition from the initial state, leading to a state with a **b**-transition. Furthermore, if '**tt**' in the above formula is replaced by '**ff**', the outcome is still 'TRUE', since there also exists an **a**-transition from the initial state to a state without a **b**-transition.

chk a.b.nil+a.c.nil [a]<b>tt

Outcome: FALSE

Indeed, there exists an **a**-transition from the initial state to a state without any **b**-transition.

chk a.nil [b]tt

Outcome: TRUE

chk a.nil [b]ff

Outcome: TRUE

Since agent **a.nil** has no **b**-transitions, anything may be stated about the (empty) set of states reachable by any **b**-transition.

6.8.5 Equivalences—Counterexamples

If two agents are not equivalent, CWB-NC can be applied to provide counterexamples.

We start with claims of strong equivalence. As a first example, consider the following CWB-NC command:

cwb-nc> eq -S bisim "a.b.nil+a.c.nil" "a.(b.nil+c.nil)"

You will obtain the outcome 'FALSE', together with the following explanation:

a.b.nil + a.c.nil satisfies: <a>[b]ff
a.(b.nil + c.nil) does not
_____

Next, we consider observation equivalence. In this connection, the above HML formalism is extended as follows:

$s \vDash [[a]]\varphi$ iff for all t with s[ext(a) > t, $t \vDash \varphi$, where ext(a) = τ*a τ*
$s \vDash \ll a \gg \varphi$ iff for some t with s[e(a) > t, $t \vDash \varphi$, where e(a) is an element of ext(a)

Now consider the following CWB-NC command:

cwb-nc> eq t.a.nil+b.nil a.nil+b.nil

The outcome is again 'FALSE', and is explained as follows:

t.a.nil + b.nil satisfies: <<eps>>[[b]]ff
a.nil + b.nil does not

_____

Here 'eps' (= ε) denotes an internal (non-observable) action.

6.8.6 More Equivalence Checking

Two agents may be strongly equivalent, provided some actions are viewed as internal, and are consequently eliminated from the original definitions of the agents concerned. In particular, note that this applies to an output action (e.g., **'ack**) and its related input action (e.g., **ack**), which participate in a parallel composition (operator '|'). This is illustrated in the following example, describing a very simple communication protocol (**VSP**):

File VSP_spec.ccs
proc VSP = put.get.VSP

_____

File VSP_imp.ccs
proc TR = put.'msg.ack.TR
proc REC = msg.get.'ack.REC
proc VSPROT = (TR|REC)\\{msg, ack}

_____

Note that the operator '\\' here refers to the elimination of the following actions.

Now load the above two files into the CCS version of CWB-NC and issue the command

eq -S bisim VSPROT VSP

You will obtain the output 'TRUE'.

6.8.7   Using the mu-Calculus

The use of HML formulas, as explained in Section 6.8.4, has its limitations. In particular, there is a problem with formulas that require a recursive definition. However, CWB-NC offers ways to overcome this problem. Namely, it also includes facilities to use a variant of the mu-calculus (for insight into essential aspects of the mu-calculus, see Reference 5). The CWB-NC mu-calculus provides facilities to check CCS-defined systems with respect to recursively defined formulas. For example, consider the problem of checking whether a system is deadlock-free. This property may be specified by the following recursive HML-formula:

DLF = <->tt ∧ [-] DLF

(for a simple explanation of this and similar recursive definitions, see Reference 4).

In particular, we are interested in the "largest possible" solution of the above recursive definition. To illustrate, assume that we wish to show that **cycle1** defined in file **cycle1.ccs** (Section 6.8.1) is deadlock-free. For this purpose we establish the following file:

File dlf.mu
prop dlf =
max X = <->tt ∧ [-]X

_____

To complete the required proof, load the above two files (**cycle1.ccs** and **dlf.mu**) into your CWB-NC system, and issue the command

chk cycle1 dlf

You will obtain the outcome 'TRUE'.
   Of course, you could try the command

chk a.b.c.nil dlf

to obtain the outcome 'FALSE'.

6.8.8   Using CTL

CWB-NC also facilitates the use of CTL (see Section 6.7) for the verification of system properties. In addition to the temporal operators defined formally in Section 6.7.1, we will also use the "weak until" operator W (mentioned in Section 6.7). Whereas the "strong until" operator U (see Section 6.7) means that fUg is valid only if 'g' eventually appears, fWg is also satisfied if 'f' holds forever.

CTL formulas can be transformed into mu-calculus formulas as follows:

AG ψ corresponds to **max X= $\psi \wedge$ [-]X**

EF ψ corresponds to **min X= $\psi \vee$ <-> X**

AF ψ corresponds to **min X= $\psi \vee$ ([-]X $\wedge$ <-> tt)**

Consequently, the preceding file *dlf.mu* (from Section 6.8.7) can be replaced by the following file:

File dlf1.mu
prop dlf1=AG <-> tt

_____

On the other hand, the following *dead.mu* file specifies the existence of a deadlock:

File dead.mu
prop dead = EF [-]ff

_____

If you go to CWB-NC, and try, for example,

chk a.b.nil dead

you will obtain 'TRUE'.

Here is an example showing the use of the "weak until" operator. The following file specifies the requirement "**a until b**", including the "**a forever**" case:

File auntilb.mu
prop auntilb =
A(<a>tt W <b>tt)

_____

If you try

chk a.a.b.c.nil auntilb

you will obtain 'TRUE'. You will also obtain 'TRUE' if you try

chk alwa auntilb

where the corresponding agent '**alwa.ccs**' is defined by **alwa = a.alwa**.

The **chk** command may also be applied to check agents with respect to CTL formulas, which are included explicitly in the command, rather than via a mu-formula. Here are some examples:

chk a.b.c.nil + b.d.nil AF<b>tt

You obtain 'TRUE'.

chk a.b.c.nil + b.d.nil AF<c>tt

This time you obtain 'FALSE'. However, if you replace **AF** by **EF** you will obtain 'TRUE'.

chk a.b.c.nil + b.d.nil AF(<c>tt V<d>tt)

The outcome becomes 'TRUE'.

chk a.b.nil + a.c.nil EF<b>tt ∧ EF<c>tt

The outcome is 'TRUE'.

chk a.b.nil + a.c.nil AF(<b>tt V <c>tt)

The outcome is again 'TRUE'.

We now assume that the following CCS file *twocy.ccs* has been loaded into your local CWB-NC system:

File twocy.ccs
proc twocy=a.b.twocy+b.c.d.twocy

————————

You may apply the command
    compile twocy
to derive the following LTS:
(0,a,1)
(0,b,2)
(1,b,0)
(2,c,3)
(3,d,0)

————————

You may apply the following commands and obtain the outcome 'TRUE':

> **chk twocy AG<->tt**   (i.e., no deadlock)
>
> **chk twocy AF<b>tt**
>
> **chk twocy EF<d>tt**
>
> **chk twocy EG(<a>tt V <b>tt)**

On the other hand, if you try

> **chk twocy AF<d>tt**

you will obtain 'FALSE'.

6.9 CCS AND CWB APPLICATION EXAMPLES

Let us now look at some simple examples illustrating the application of CWB-NC.

6.9.1 The CCS XCEL-Circuit Example

6.9.1.1 The CCS Approach   We consider the circuit XCEL, the block diagram of which is shown in Fig. 6.3. For details about the CEL and XOR components, recall Chapter 3.

The following are the CCS files describing the implementation and defining the specification of the XCEL circuit:

File XCELimpl.ccs
proc xor = a.'y.xor + b.'y.xor
proc cel = y.c.z.cel + c.y.z.cel
proc XCELimpl = (xor|cel)\{y}

_____

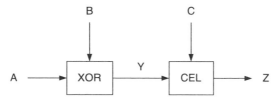

Figure 6.3   Block diagram of circuit XCEL.

File XCELspec.ccs
proc XCEL = a.c.z.XCEL + c.a.z.XCEL + b.c.z.XCEL + c.b.z.XCEL

To check whether L(XCEL) is contained in L(XCELimpl), we load the above two files into our CWB-NC system, and issue the command

le -S may XCEL XCELimpl

which gives the result 'TRUE'.

We may use the '**compile**' command to get LTS-based representations of **XCEL** and **XCELimpl**. For example, the outcome of the command '**compile XCEL**' is as follows:

(0,a,1)
(0,b,1)
(0,c,2)
(0,c,3)
(1,c,4)
(2,a,4)
(3,b,4)
(4,z,0)

We may apply CTL within CWB-NC, to confirm that XCELimpl is dead-lock-free. If we issue the command

chk XCELimpl AG<->tt

we obtain 'TRUE'. Thus **XCELimpl** is indeed deadlock-free.

On the other hand, if we issue the command

chk XCELimpl EF[-]ff

we obtain 'FALSE', indicating that **XCELimpl** has no dead state.

The following are some more examples of applying CTL (within CWB-NC) to **XCELimpl**:

chk XCELimpl AG<z>tt

The outcome is 'FALSE.' Indeed, there are states without an outgoing '**z**' transition. On the other hand, if we issue the command

chk XCELimpl AF<z>tt

we obtain 'TRUE', and indeed the transition '**z**' is eventually reachable from every path.

6.9.1.2 Comparing the CCS Approach with the LOTOS Approach

It turns out that the preceding CCS approach is quite similar to the corresponding LOTOS approach. We now present the files *XCELimpl.lotos* and *XCELsp.lotos*, which "similate" the above files *XCELimpl.ccs* and *XCELspec.ccs*:

File XCELimpl.lotos
specification XCELimpl[a,b,c,z]:noexit behaviour
        hide y in
        xor[a,b,y]|[y]|cel[y,c,z]
where
  process xor[a,b,z]:noexit:=
      a;z;xor[a,b,z] [] b;z;xor[a,b,z]
  endproc
  process cel[a,b,z]:noexit:=
      a;b;z;cel[a,b,z] [] b;a;z;cel[a,b,z]
  endproc
endspec

File XCELsp.lotos
specification XCELsp[a,b,c,z]:noexit behaviour
        XCELsp[a,b,c,z]
 where
   process XCELsp[a,b,c,z]:noexit:=
      a;c;z;XCELsp[a,b,c,z][]c;a;z;XCELsp[a,b,c,z][]
      b;c;z;XCELsp[a,b,c,z][]c;b;z;XCELsp[a,b,c,z]
   endproc
endspec

We suggest that you generate the corresponding aut-files, and apply the following CADP command (provided you have the relevant version of CADP):

aldebaran - oord XCELsp.aut XCELimpl.aut

You should obtain 'TRUE', confirming an observation preorder relation between the relevant specification and implementation.

6.9.2   The CCS CEL3-Circuit Example

In Section 3.1.2 we introduced the 3-input CEL-circuit, indicating its specification **cel3spec1**, and its implementation **CEL3[A,B,C,Z]**. We now present the corresponding CCS representations.

The specification as formulated in the CCS file is as follows:

File cel3.ccs
proc cel3 = a.b.c.z.cel3 + a.c.b.z.cel3 + b.a.c.z.cel3 + b.c.a.z.cel3 +
                c.a.b.z.cel3 + c.b.a.z.cel3

——————————

The implementation is defined in the following CCS file:

File C3.ccs
proc cel1 = a.b.'y.cel1 + b.a.'y.cel1
proc cel2 = y.c.z.cel2 + c.y.z.cel2
proc C3 = (cel1 | cel2)\{y}

——————————

After you load the above two files into your CWB-NC system, you may proceed as follows. Issue the command

le -S trace cel3 C3

You will obtain 'TRUE', confirming the relevant language containment.

Applying the '**compile**' command to **cel3** and **C3** will produce the corresponding LTSs. For example, the outcome of the command '**compile cel3**' is as follows:

(0,a,1)
(0,a,2)
(0,b,3)
(0,b,4)
(0,c,5)
(0,c,6)
(1,b,7)
(2,c,8)
(3,a,7)
(4,c,9)
(5,a,8)
(6,b,9)
(7,c,10)
(8,b,10)

(9,a,10)
(10,z,0)

———————

You may also confirm that the properties applicable to **XCELimpl**, as shown in Section 6.9.1, also apply to **C3**.

EXERCISES

6.1 Below we list two equivalences, using Blot. Formulate each equivalence by means of CCS agents and verify them using CWB-NC. In particular, show that the equivalence in (a) is strong, whereas that in (b) is not.

(a) **tick;tick;clock = clock** where **clock =** ***[tick]**

(b) **(a!;b;\$ || a?;c;\$)\{a}= b;c;\$ [] c;b;\$**. Recall that '!' denotes 'output' and '?' denotes 'input'.

6.2 Convert the agent '**a.b.nil | c.nil**' into a strongly equivalent agent without the ' **|** ' operator. Use CWB-NC to confirm your solution.

6.3 Convert the following two Blot processes into corresponding CCS agents. Use CWB-NC to show that the two agents are not equivalent. Indicate suitable distinguishing properties.

agent1 = a;b;\$ || c;\$

agent2 = c;a;b;\$ [] a;c;b;\$ [] a;b;c;\$

6.4 Consider the property "eventually '**a**' will appear". Formulate this property:

(a) as CCS **eva.mu** formula, using CTL;

(b) same as (a), but without the use of CTL.

6.5 Use CCS to formulate the specification and implementation of XOR3 (see Section 3.2.2). Then proceed as in Sections 6.9.1.1 and 6.9.1.2.

6.10 FURTHER READING

For further insight into the material of this chapter, we again recommend the work contained in Reference 4. As indicated earlier, Reference 6 also contains very helpful information about CWB-NC.

6.11 SELECTED SOLUTIONS

6.1 **(a)** Define **clock.ccs** by

$$\text{proc clock} = \text{tick.clock}$$

Then go to CWB-NC and issue the command

$$\text{eq -S bisim tick.tick.clock clock}$$

You will obtain 'TRUE'.

(b) Within CWB-NC issue the command

$$\text{eq('a.b.nil | a.c.nil)} \backslash \{a\} \ \text{b.c.nil+c.b.nil}$$

You will obtain 'TRUE'.

However, the two agents are not strongly equivalent. The first agent satisfies **<t>tt**, but the second does not.

6.2 The required agent appears as the second agent in the following CWB-NC command:

$$\text{eq -S bisim a.b.nil | c.nil a.(b.c.nil + c.b.nil) + c.a.b.nil}$$

The outcome of this command is 'TRUE', confirming that the two agents are strongly equivalent.

Alternatively, you may apply the CWB-NC command '**compile**' to the two agents, producing identical LTSs.

6.3 Go to your CWB-NC system and issue the command

$$\text{eq a.b.nil | c.nil c.a.b.nil + a.c.b.nil + a.b.c.nil}$$

You will get 'FALSE', together with an explanation stating that **agent1** satisfies **[[a]] <<b>>tt** whereas **agent2** does not.

6.4 **(a)** <u>**eval.mu**</u>

    prop AF <a> tt

(b) <u>**eva.mu**</u>
    prop eva =
        min X<-> tt $\wedge$ [-a]X

6.12 REFERENCES

1. Milner R. A calculus of communicating systems. Springer, 1980.
2. Milner R. Communication and concurrency. Prentice-Hall, 1989.
3. Hoare CA. Communicating sequential processes. Prentice-Hall, 1985.
4. Bruns G. Distributed systems analysis with CCS. Prentice-Hall, 1997.
5. Clarke EM, Grumberg O, Peled DA. Model checking. MIT Press, 1999.
6. The Concurrency Workbench of New Century (CWB-NC), June 2000. http://www.cs.sunysb.edu/~cwb/.

## CHAPTER 7

Verification of Modular Asynchronous Circuits

7.1 ABOUT ASYNCHRONOUS CIRCUITS

Asynchronous circuits are sequential circuits that operate without any global clock control. In an asynchronous circuit each component starts its computation as soon as all the required data are available and transmits its outputs to the next components as soon as its computation is completed. In synchronous (clock-controlled) circuits the transfer of data is delayed until the occurrence of the next clock signal. Thus an asynchronous circuit may, in principle, be faster than its synchronous counterpart. Furthermore, the asynchronous approach assists in reducing power consumption. Therefore asynchronous circuits are of particular interest in connection with portable devices and airborne systems.

However, it turns out that synchronous circuits are easier to design than asynchronous ones. In recent years there has been a great surge of interest in asynchronous designs, in view of the above advantages. Both the practical and the theoretical aspects of such designs are being extensively investigated. For more details, see Reference 1.

7.1.1 Modular Asynchronous Circuits

In this text we are particularly interested in *modular* asynchronous circuits, which are designed as a composition of *basic modules*. Such modules are more complex than simple gates; their correct behavior is to be assured by suitable circuit design rather than by logic design. A special class of such

Verification of Systems and Circuits Using LOTOS, Petri Nets, and CCS, by Michael Yoeli and Rakefet Kol
Copyright © 2008 John Wiley & Sons, Inc.

circuits is formed by *delay-insensitive* circuits, the correct behavior of which does not depend on delays either of their components or of their interconnections. They are easier to design and to verify than arbitrary asynchronous circuits.

7.1.2 Edge-Based (Dynamic) Versus Level-Based Behavior

As pointed out in Chapter 1, the event-based approach to systems and circuits is preferably applicable to the specification and verification of asynchronous circuits. Hence all our discussions of asynchronous circuits apply the event-based approach. In this chapter we prefer to use the Boolean variables F ("false") and T ("true"), rather than the binary variables 0 and 1 used in Chapter 3. In most cases we use capital letters to denote Boolean variables, and the corresponding lower-case letters to denote level changes ("transitions").

7.2 XOR-GATES

In Section 3.2 we introduced various XOR-gates, using Blot, wherever applicable. We now wish to resume our exposition, using the tools introduced in Chapters 4–6. We start with a LOTOS specification of the 2-input XOR-gate, assuming that it is started in one of its stable states $Z = A\#B$. Here A and B are the Boolean inputs, Z is the Boolean output, and '#' denotes the exclusive-or operator. Recall that $F\#T=T\#F=T$ and $F\#F=T\#T=F$.

7.2.1 LOTOS Representation of XOR-Gate

The LOTOS representation of a 2-input XOR-gate is given in the following file:

File xor.lotos
specification xor[a,b,z]:noexit behaviour
     xor[a,b,z]
where
  process xor[a,b,z]:noexit:=
     a;z;xor[a,b,z] [] b;z;xor[a,b,z]
  endproc
endspec

————————

7.2.2 Petri Net Representation of XOR-Gate

The following file is a PETRIFY-based representation of the same 2-input XOR-gate:

File xor.net
.model xor.net
.inputs a b
.outputs z
.graph
p0 a b
a p1
b p1
p1 z
z p0
.marking {p0}
.end

7.2.3 CCS Representation of XOR-Gate

Our third approach to representing the 2-input XOR-gate is by using CCS representation, as defined in the following file:

File xor.ccs
proc xor = a.z.xor + b.z.xor

Each of the above representations is easily converted into an LTS (Labeled Transition System). With respect to LOTOS, we apply CADP (see Section 4.8). With respect to Petri nets, we use the **write_sg** facility of PETRIFY (see Section 5.3). As for CCS, we apply the **compile** facility of CWB-NC (see Section 6.8).

EXERCISE

7.1 Show that all the above three approaches yield the same LTS.

7.3 CEL-CIRCUIT

We introduced CEL-circuits ("C-Elements" (2)) informally in Section 3.1, using our Blot approach. We now turn again to the use of the tools of Chapters 4–6, starting again with the relevant LOTOS representation.

7.3.1   LOTOS Representation of CEL-Circuit

The LOTOS representation of a CEL-circuit is given in the following file:

File cel.lotos
specification cel[a,b,z]:noexit behaviour
        cel[a,b,z]
where
    process cel[a,b,z]:noexit:=
        a;b;z;cel[a,b,z] [] b;a;z;cel[a,b,z]
    endproc
endspec

Note that the above specification assumes $A = B = Z$ as the initial condition.

7.3.2   Petri Net Representation of CEL-Circuit

The following file is a suitably reduced PETRIFY representation of a CEL-circuit:

File cel.net
.model cel.net
.inputs a b
.outputs z
.graph
a z
b z
z a b
.marking {<z,a> <z,b>}
.end

7.3.3   CCS Representation of CEL-Circuit

The corresponding CCS-file for representing a CEL-circuit in CCS is as follows:

File cel.ccs
proc cel = a.b.z.cel + b.a.z.cel

EXERCISE

7.2 For each of the above three representations, derive the corresponding LTS, and confirm that the three LTSs obtained are isomorphic.

7.4 OTHER MODULES

In addition to the XOR and CEL modules discussed so far in this chapter, we now turn to some additional modules of interest.

7.4.1 Inverter

The INVERTER, with a Boolean input A and Boolean output Z, is stable iff $Z = \sim A$. If started in the (unstable) state $Z = A$, its event-based (dynamic) behavior may be specified by the Blot expression

$$INV[a,z] = INV = \ ^*[z;a]$$

Given some modular network, we assume that the environment assures that each module adheres to the following "fundamental mode restriction" (which we have already formulated in Section 3.2.1, in connection with the XOR-module):

- In a stable condition an input may be applied.
- In an unstable condition no input may be applied, but an output must occur.

7.4.2 ICEL-Element

The ICEL-circuit is obtained from the CEL-circuit by connecting an INVERTER to the A-input of the CEL-circuit. It can be specified by the following Blot expression, which relates **ICEL** to **CEL**:

$$ICEL = b;z;CEL$$

Note that ICEL can also be expressed by

$$ICEL[a,b,z] = \ ^+[b;z] \ \| \ ^*[z;a]$$

EXERCISE

7.3 (a) Define **ICEL** using LOTOS/CADP and produce a (reduced) LTS.

(b) Define **ICEL** using CCS. Apply CWB-NC to derive the corresponding LTS.

(c) Compare the two LTSs.

7.4.3 TOGGLE

You have already met toggles informally (using Blot) in Section 3.3. Recall the definition of the 2-output **TOGGLE** (**TOG**) with an input A and outputs Y, Z. Its (dynamic) behavior may be described by the following Blot expression, starting, say, at the initial state $A = Y = Z = F$:

$$\text{TOGGLE}[a,y,z] = \text{TOGGLE} = {}^{*}[a;y;a;z]$$

For the application of Petri nets and PETRIFY to the specification of TOGGLE, see Example 5.2 in Section 5.4.

EXERCISE

7.4 Specify **TOGGLE** by LOTOS as well as by Petri net. Compare the relevant LTSs.

7.4.4 CALL

A CALL module is intended for application in systems where two processing units share the same computing device. The outside connections of this module are shown in Fig. 7.1. The following is a Blot specification of its dynamic behavior, starting from the initial state "all F":

$$\text{CALL} = {}^{*}[r1;r;d;d1\,[\,]\,r2;r;d;d2]$$

Alternative specifications can be found in Reference 3.

Figure 7.1 Module CALL interface.

EXERCISES

7.5 Construct a net (**call.net**) specifying the above behavior of **CALL**.

7.6 Specify **CALL** in CCS, using CWB-NC.

7.5 MODULE EXTENSIONS

In Chapter 3 we introduced XOR-gates and CEL-circuits with more than two inputs. Below we further discuss such extensions. In the sequel we discuss the implementation of such extended modules by means of 2-input modules.

7.5.1 XORk ($k > 2$) Modules

In Section 3.3 we used Blot to describe the specification and implementation of the 3-input XOR-gate. XOR-gates with more than three inputs may be handled in a similar way.

EXERCISES

7.7 Use the three approaches—LOTOS, Petri nets, and CCS—to obtain suitable representations of the specification and implementation of the XOR3 module.

7.8 (a) Use Blot to describe the tree-format of a 4-input XOR-gate.

(b) Extend the representations from Exercise 7.7 to the 4-input XOR-gate.

7.5.2 CEL k ($k > 2$) Modules

In Section 3.1 we used Blot to discuss the 3- and 4-input CEL-circuits. The following is a PETRIFY specification of the 3-input CEL-circuit; the assumption is again that initially $A = B = C = Z$:

File cel3spec.net
.model cel3spec.net
.inputs a b c
.outputs z
.graph
a z
b z
c z

z a b c
.marking {<z,a> <z,b> <z,c>}
.end

CELk-nets, $k > 3$, are specified in a similar way.

EXERCISE

7.9   Define **cel3spec** using LOTOS. Show that the LTSs corresponding to **cel3spec.net** and **cel3spec.lotos** are isomorphic.

7.5.3   TOGk ($k > 2$)

We introduced k-output toggles for $k = 2, 3, 4$ in Section 3.3. The extension to a k-output toggle ($k > 4$) is straightforward. For example, TOG5 is defined in Blot as follows:

$$\textbf{TOG5[a, y1, y2, y3, y4, y5] = *[a;y1;a;y2;a;y3;a;y4;a;y5]}.$$

EXERCISE

7.10 (a)   Design a uniquely labeled net tog3.net, specifying **TOG3**.
  (b)   Specify **TOG3** using LOTOS.
  (c)   Specify **TOG3** using CCS.
  (d)   Show that the LTSs corresponding to (a), (b), and (c) are isomorphic.

7.6   MODULAR NETWORKS

In Section 3.5 we illustrated the composition of modules (modular network) by a particular example. In general, a modular network is obtained by suitably interconnecting a finite number of modules. The modules of such a network must adhere to the following restriction.

If P is an input of any module, there may be at most one module with P as output. In such a case the output P of this particular module is connected to every input P occurring in any other module. Such an interconnection P may be declared either as an output node of the network or as an internal node. If the module output P is connected to more than one module, such a connection is referred to as a **fork**.

7.7 REALIZATIONS

7.7.1 Introduction to Realization

We now wish to discuss the connections between a process specifying a *behavior* and a modular network (an *implementation*), which (in a suitable sense) "satisfies" the given behavior specification. We will use the term *realization* to refer to the relationship between a specification and its implementation. We introduce various types of realization and discuss corresponding verification approaches. In the sequel we illustrate the verification of some of the extended modules introduced in Section 7.5. Furthermore, we refer to some publications indicating how various realization concepts are related to each other.

7.7.2 Type-A Realization

In the extreme case the specification **spec** and its implementation **impl** are strongly equivalent. We refer to this type of realization as a *Type-A realization*.

As an example, consider the following Blot description of a specification and its implementation:

$$\textbf{spec1} = (\textbf{*[up;x]} \parallel \textbf{*[x;y]}) \parallel \textbf{*[y;down]}$$

$$\textbf{impl1} = \textbf{ICEL[y,up,x]} \parallel \textbf{ICEL[down,x,y]}$$

We wish to prove that **spec1 = impl1**, i.e., that the two are strongly equivalent.

Proposition 7.1

$$\textbf{impl1} = \textbf{spec1}$$

Proof

$$\textbf{spec1} = (\textbf{*[up;x]} \parallel \textbf{*[x;y]}) \parallel \textbf{*[y;down]}$$
$$= \textbf{*[up;x]} \parallel \textbf{*[x;y]} \parallel \textbf{*[x;y]} \parallel \textbf{*[y;down]} =$$
$$= \textbf{ICEL[y,up,x]} \parallel \textbf{ICEL[down,x,y]} =$$
$$= \textbf{impl1}$$

EXERCISE

7.11   Use CADP to prove Proposition 7.1.

7.7.2.1 Type-A1 Realization   Frequently, the specification **spec** and its implementation **impl** are not strongly equivalent, but are observation-equivalent. We refer to such a case as a *Type-A1 realization*. However, this type of equivalence does not prevent the undesirable case where **impl** contains a *livelock*, i.e., a cycle of internal events. To illustrate this point, consider the following two Blot processes:

$$PX\_A := *[a;z]$$

$$PX\_B := *[i;i\ [\ ]\ a;z]$$

You can easily verify that **PX_A == PX_B**, i.e., they are observation-equivalent. However, **PX_B** contains an undesirable i-cycle. The existence of such an i-cycle can evidently be detected by constructing the relevant process graph.

EXERCISE

7.12   Use CADP to verify that **PX_A = = PX_B**.

7.7.3 Type-B Realization

We now turn to a quite general situation, where the implementation **impl** may differ considerably from its specification **spec**. The following are examples of such differences:

(a) **impl** is more powerful than **spec**, i.e., the implementation may perform activities not required by the specification.

(b) the implementation may behave "non-deterministically", while the specification excludes such a behavior. Non-deterministic behavior is meant here in a sense that *"The application of an input to some state of the implementation may lead to two or more states."*

As an example, let (using Blot) **spec** = *[a;z] and **impl** = *[a;z] [] *[a;i;z]. Nevertheless, we consider **impl** to be a "realization" of **spec**.

We now wish to formalize the particular type of realization we have in mind. We start by formalizing the relevant concepts of implementation (called here a "Circuit Transition System" or CTS) and its specification. We then formalize the corresponding concept of "realization", which we refer to as a *Type-B realization*. The material is taken from Reference 4. For a related approach, see Chapter 11 of Reference 5.

Definition B1   A *Circuit Transition System* CT is a 6-tuple CT = (inCT, outCT, intCT, QCT, fCT, q0CT).

> inCT is a finite set of input symbols. An input symbol represents an input node of the relevant circuit, as well as a change of the logic level (i.e., from 0 to 1, or from 1 to 0) at the corresponding node.
>
> Similarly, outCT and intCT are finite sets of output symbols and internal symbols, respectively. Output symbols and internal symbols represent corresponding circuit nodes, as well as their level changes.
>
> The sets inCT, outCT, and intCT are mutually disjoint.
>
> We denote aCT = inCT ∪ outCT ∪ intCT.
>
> QCT is a finite set of states.
>
> fCT, the next-state function, is a partial function from QCT × aCT into QCT.
>
> q0CT ∈ QCT is the initial state of CT.

We postulate that all states in QCT are reachable from the initial state.

Let CT be a circuit transition system, as defined above. CT may be viewed as an acceptor automaton with aCT as its alphabet. We consider every state of QCT to be an accepting state, and denote by L(CT) the corresponding language.

Let $w \in$ L(CT). We denote by w\intCT the restriction of w to the alphabet inCT ∪ outCT, and set L(CT)\intCT = {w\intCT|w ∈ L(CT)}.

We denote by CT\ the automaton obtained from CT by replacing its internal symbols by ε. Evidently, CT\ may be non-deterministic, although CT has been defined as a deterministic system.

Definition B2   A *Circuit Specification* S is a CTS, where intCT= Ø. We set S = (inS, outS, QS, fS, q0S).

The language L(S) is defined similarly to the above definition of L(CT). The following definition is intended to formalize the intuitive concept "CT is a realization of S".

Definition B3   Let S = (inS, outS, QS, fS, q0S) be a specification and CT be a circuit transition system, CT = (inCT, outCT, intCT, QCT, fCT, q0CT).

We say that CT is a *Type-B realization* of S (notation: $CT \models /B \ S$) iff the following conditions are satisfied (note that we use ';' to denote concatenation):

(**Req B1**) $inCT = inS$

(**Req B2**) $outCT = outS$

(**Req B3**) $L(S) \subseteq L(CT)\backslash intCT$

(**Req B4**)   Assume $w \in L(S)$, $z \in outS$, $w';z \in L(CT)$ and $w'\backslash intCT = w$. Then $w;z \in L(S)$.

(**Req B5**)   Assume $w1;w2 \in L(S)$, and that there exists $w' \in L(CT)$, such that $w'\backslash intCT = w1$. Then there exists w'' such that $w''\backslash intCT = w2$ and $w';w'' \in L(CT)$.

(**Req B6**)   Let $w \in L(S)$, $w' \in L(CT)$, and $w'\backslash intCT = w$. Then there exists a positive integer k such that for any word $w'' \in (intCT)^*$, $w';w'' \in L(CT)$ implies $length(w'') < k$.

Clearly, if $CT\backslash$ is deterministic, requirement (Req B5) is implied by requirement (Req B3), i.e., requirement (Req B5) becomes redundant.

Informally, the above Definition B3 may be motivated as follows:

(a) The input and output symbols of CT are assumed to coincide with inS and outS, respectively (requirements (Req B1) and (Req B2)).

(b) We expect the realization to be capable of producing for any signal sequence specified by L(S) a sequence that, after deletion of its internal symbols, will be equal to the above signal sequence. CT may even be capable of performing more than required by S (requirement (Req B3)).

(c) The realization may not produce any "undesirable" outputs (requirement (Req B4)).

(d) Requirement (Req B5) is rather evident; as mentioned above, this requirement is redundant, if $CT\backslash$ is deterministic.

(e) A word of the realization which reduces to a word in L(S), cannot be continued by an infinite sequence of internal signals (requirement (Req B6)).

7.7.4   Type-C Realization

In this type of realization we assume that the circuit specification and its implementation are formulated by Blot processes, or, alternatively, by Basic-LOTOS programs. Assume now that both the circuit implementation **impl** and its specification **spec** are represented by Blot processes.

(*Req C1*)   **Act(spec)** is divided into **input(spec)** and **output(spec)**. All actions of **spec** are observable. Also, all actions of **impl** are observable. **Act(impl)** is divided into **input(impl)**, **output(impl)**, and **internal**. We postulate that **input(impl)= input(spec)** and **output(impl) = output(spec)**.

(*Req C2*)   **impl ‖ spec == spec**, where == denotes observation equivalence. Thus, if the inputs of **impl** are activated in accordance with **spec**, the outputs produced by **impl** will also be in accordance with **spec**.

(*Req C3*)   **impl\internal** (obtained by replacing all actions in **internal** by **i**) contains no i-cycle (i.e., is livelock-free; see Section 7.7.2.1).

(*Req C4*)   If **impl** is more powerful than **spec**, then **impl** may produce "undesirable" outputs. To be more precise, let **seq** be a sequence of events appearing in both **spec** and **impl**. Let **z** be an output and let **seq;z** be an event sequence of **impl**. Then we expect **seq;z** to also be an event sequence of **spec**. Otherwise, this occurrence of the output **z** is *undesirable*.

(*Req C5*)   **impl** is *deadlock-free with respect to* **spec**. This requirement may be formulated as follows. If **seq** are action sequences in both **impl** and **spec**, and **seq** can be continued in **spec**, then **seq** can also be continued in **impl**.

Note that requirement (Req C5) follows from requirement (Req C2). Nevertheless, we consider it of interest to include it in our listing of requirements (cf. Chapter 11 of Reference 5).

The following example shows that requirement (Req C4) is independent of requirement (Req C2).

Example 7.1   Let

$$spec = *[a;b;z]$$

$$impl = *[a;(b;z\ []\ z)]$$

Here **a** and **b** are input signals and **z** is the output signal. In this example (Req C2) is satisfied, but (Req C4) is not. Namely, **impl** admits the sequence **a;z**, thus producing an undesirable output. To detect that (Req C4) is not satisfied, we may use CADP and make use of the fact that the operator '‖' does not require synchronization on **i**. Hence we may proceed as follows. We transform the Blot process impl\internal into the aut-file impl.aut and convert this file into file **nimpl.aut**, by replacing **z** by **i;z**. Next, we convert the file **nimpl.aut** into the corresponding LOTOS file **nimpl.lotos**. Then we generate the file **ver.lotos = nimpl.lotos ‖ spec.lotos**, where **spec.lotos** is the LOTOS representation of **spec**. By applying CADP (see manual!), we find that **ver.lotos** contains a deadlock. This indicates that (Req C4) is not satisfied.

7.7.5 Type-D Realization

In this section we introduce an alternative approach to the notion of realization, based on Petri nets. In particular, we again deal with the assumption that the implementation is more powerful than the specification.

Let us assume that we are given a specification of an asynchronous circuit or system in the form of a labeled Petri net SPN. The labeling alphabet of SPN is partitioned into two parts: input labels and output labels. Similarly, the edge-based behavior of a relevant implementation is represented by a labeled Petri net IMPN. Its labeling alphabet is partitioned into three parts: input labels, output labels, and internal labels.

We impose the following restrictions on this approach; as will be illustrated in the sequel, the restrictions considered are adhered to by a large class of practical examples:

(Da)   SPN and IMPN are both live and safe.

(Db)   The input labels of both nets coincide, and so do their output labels.

(Dc)   The two nets have only one output; the corresponding label appears only once in each net.

Informally, we might say that the net IMPN realizes the given specification net SPN, if IMPN "behaves" as specified by SPN, similarly to (Req C2) and (Req C4) of Section 7.7.4. More precisely, we formulate the following two definitions:

Definition D1 The *Environment Restriction Net* env.SPnet of a given specification net SPN is obtained from SPN by omitting all the edges incoming to output transitions, i.e., transitions labeled by output labels.

Definition D2 Let IMPN, SPN, and env.SPnet be as defined above. IMPN is a *Type-D realization* of SPN (notation: IMPN $\models$ SPN) iff the following conditions are met:

(1) (env.SPnet ‖ IMPN) is a safe net and is observation-equivalent with SPN.

(2) IMPN does not contain a cycle of internal labels.

Frequently, it will be convenient to use the following definition instead of Definition D2:

Definition D3 Let IMPN, SPN be as defined above. IMPN is a *Type-D1 realization* of SPN iff the following conditions are met:

(1) SPnet ‖ IMPN is a safe net and is observation-equivalent with SPN.
(2) IMPN does not contain a cycle of internal labels.

In general, this definition is easier to apply than Definition D2. In order to show that IMPN |= SPN we have to use ad hoc methods to show that IMPN does not produce undesirable outputs.

7.7.5.1 *Extended Type-D Realizations*

The above approach is easily extended to the case where the implementation is represented by a modular network. In this case we first convert the given modular network into the corresponding Petri net IMPN.

7.7.6 DI Realization

In this section we introduce the concept of DI realization and indicate that all the realizations discussed so far are indeed DI.

One way of defining DI is by means of the foam rubber wrapper constraint (see page 329 of Reference 5). This constraint requires that "we must be able to attach arbitrary delays to the input and output wires of any DI-circuit, and the new circuit must behave (externally) in the same way as the original circuit."

The above requirement could be restricted by replacing "arbitrary delays" by "unit delays". Such a "unit-delay extension" of a given modular circuit is easily formulated using either net or process models, and can be checked against the above requirement. One easily verifies that all the realizations introduced in this chapter are indeed DI.

7.8 VERIFICATION OF EXTENDED MODULES

A variety of extended modules, with three or more inputs, have been introduced both in Chapter 3 as well as in the preceding sections of this chapter. We now turn to the formal verification of such extended modules. In particular, we wish to apply the various tools introduced in Chapters 4–6 to show that implementations of such extended modules are indeed realizations of the relevant specifications.

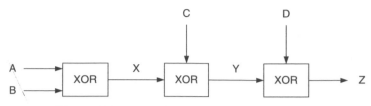

Figure 7.2   Cascade implementation of XOR4.

7.8.1   Verification of XOR*k* (*k* > 2) Modules

We already discussed some aspects of XOR3 modules in Sections 3.2.2 and 7.5.1. We now turn to the verification of the general case $k > 2$.

7.8.1.1   Implementation of XORk   A XORk ($k > 2$) module can be built either by a cascade of XOR modules or by a tree of XOR modules. A cascade implementation of XOR4 is shown in Fig. 7.2. We use the following (Blot-based) text version to describe Fig. 7.2:

XOR4_IMP[A,B,C,D,Z] =

(XOR[A,B,X] ‖ XOR[X,C,Y] ‖ XOR[Y,D,Z]) \ {X.Y}

Below we discuss in detail tree-type implementations of XOR4 and their specification and verification. The above cascade implementation can easily be handled in a similar way.

7.8.1.2   Verification of XORk Using Petri Nets and PETRIFY   We now illustrate the use of Petri nets and PETRIFY in the specification, implementation, and verification of XORk modules.

As an example, we consider the following XOR4 module using PETRIFY:

File xor4.net
.model xor4.net
.inputs a b c d
.outputs z
.graph
p0 a b c d
a p1
b p1
c p1
d p1

```
p1 z
z p0
.marking {p0}
.end
```

_____

The XOR4 module can be implemented by three XOR modules connected in a tree formation, as shown in Fig. 7.3. We wish to show that Fig. 7.3 represents a Type-D realization of the above xor4.net specification. For this purpose, we generate the net

$$\textbf{xor4ver.net} = \textbf{IMPN} \parallel \textbf{env.SPnet}$$

where **IMPN** is the net corresponding to Fig. 7.3 and **env.SPnet** is the net defined in Section 7.7.5. The net **xor4ver.net** is as follows:

File xor4ver.net
```
.model xor4ver.net
.inputs a b c d
.outputs z
.dummy x y
.graph
#xor[a,b,x]
p0 a b
a p1
b p1
p1 x
x p0
#xor[c,d,y]
p2 c d
c p3
d p3
p3 y
y p2
#xor[x,y,z]
p4 x y
x p5
y p5
p5 z
z p4
#env
```

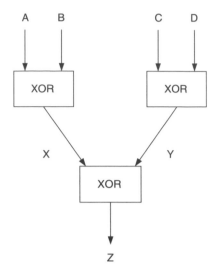

Figure 7.3 Tree implementation of XOR4.

```
z p6
p6 a b c d
.marking {p0 p2 p4 p6}
.end
```

Next, we wish to hide the dummy variables x and y. This is achieved by issuing the command

petrify -hide.dummy xor4ver.net

The outcome coincides with the above specification net *xor4.net*!

7.8.1.3 *Verification of XORk Using LOTOS and CADP* Using Blot, we define

XOR4.sp = a;z;XOR4.sp [] b;z;XOR4.sp [] c;z;XOR4.sp [] d;z;XOR4.sp

XOR4.impl = ((XOR[a,b,r] ||| XOR[c,d,s]) | [r,s] | XOR[r,s,z]) \ {r,s}

EXERCISE

7.13 (a) Use CADP to show that **XOR4.impl** "covers" (see Section 2.7.1) **XOR4.sp**.

(b) Use CADP to prove that **XOR4.impl** is a Type-C realization of **XOR4.sp**.

7.8.1.4 Verification of XORk Using CCS and CWB-NC

EXERCISE

7.14 Use CWB-NC to show that the language L(**XOR4.sp**) is contained in L(**XOR4.impl**).

7.8.2 Verification of CELk (k > 2) Modules

7.8.2.1 Implementation of CELk
For earlier discussions of the CEL3 and CEL4 circuits, see Sections 3.1 and 7.5. A cascade-implementation of CEL3 is indicated in Fig. 3.2. We use the following text version to describe Fig. 3.2:

$$\mathbf{CEL3IMPL[A,B,C,Z] = CEL[A,B,Y] \mid [Y] \mid CEL[Y,C,Z]\backslash\{Y\}}$$

Thus, Y is to be viewed as an internal (hidden) signal.

To informally verify that Fig. 3.2 represents a Type-D realization of the net *cel3spec.net* (Section 7.5.2), we start from a defined initial state, namely $A = B = C = Y = Z$, and show that changing all the three inputs in any order will yield a change of the output.

7.8.2.2 Verification of CELk Using Petri Nets and PETRIFY
Recall now the definitions of Type-D realization from Section 7.7.5. To ensure that requirement (1) of Definition D2 is satisfied, consider the following net, described using PETRIFY:

File cel3ver.net
.model cel3ver.net
.inputs a b c
.outputs z
.dummy y
.graph
#cel[a,b,y]
a y
b y
y a b
#cel[y,c,z]

y z
c z
z y c
#env.SPnet
z a b
.marking (<y,a> <y,b> <z,a> <z,b> <z,c> <z,y>)
.end

_____

Note that **env.SPnet** is obtained from *cel3spec.net* of Section 7.5.2 by omitting the arcs <a,z>, <b,z>, <c,z>. Furthermore, we omit <z,c>, since this arc already appears in #cel[y,c,z].

The above net, which is evidently a marked graph, is easily drawn by hand and converted into a state graph, isomorphic to the state graph obtainable from cel3.net (i.e., the two state graphs differ only in their state labels).

Alternatively, we may use PETRIFY for the comparison of the two nets. Namely, we issue the command

petrify -hide.dummy cel3ver.net -o out.net

The resulting *out.net* coincides with the above specification net cel3.net. Hence requirement (1) of Definition D2 is satisfied. Requirement (2) is very easily confirmed.

It follows that the network of Fig. 3.2 is indeed a Type-D realization of the specification represented by cel3spec.net of Section 7.5.2.

7.8.2.3 *Verification of CELk Using LOTOS and CADP*

EXERCISE

7.15   Use CADP to define cel3.spec and to verify that Fig. 3.2 represents a Type-C realization of cel3.spec.

7.8.2.4 *Verification of CELk Using CCS and CWB-NC*

EXERCISE

7.16   Define cel3.spec and cel3.impl, using CCS. Then use CWB-NC to show that L(cel3.spec) is contained in L(cel3.impl).

7.8.3 Verification of TOG*k* (*k* > 2) Modules

In Section 7.5.3 we mentioned that TOG3 may be specified by the Blot expression

$$^*[a;w;a;x;a;y]$$

Various methods of implementing TOG*k* (*k* > 2) are presented in Reference 3, using TOG and XOR modules. For TOG3, the methods of Reference 3 yield the following implementation, presented in Blot:

TOG3.impl[a,w,x,y] =

XOR[a,z,b] || (TOG[b,r,s] || (TOG[r,w,y] ||| TOG[s,x,z]))\ {b,r,s,z}

EXERCISE

7.17 (a) Use CADP to prove the above implementation of TOG3.

    (b) Use PETRIFY to obtain a uniquely labeled net tog3.net.

7.9 VERIFICATION OF PARALLEL CONTROL STRUCTURES

A large class of digital networks can be decomposed into a (parallel) control structure and a data structure, consisting of devices controlled by the control part of the system. The verification of the parallel control structures is another example of using the verification methods that we have presented.

For example, consider the system shown in Fig. 7.4. This system consists of a control part C, and two controlled devices S_1 and S_2. A functional decomposition of the control part is shown in Fig. 7.5.

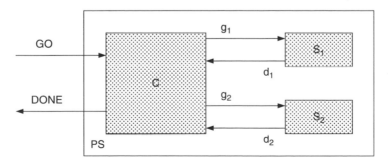

Figure 7.4 Parallel hardware system PS.

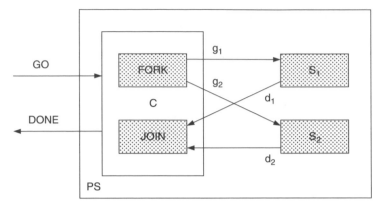

Figure 7.5   Functional decomposition of control device C.

Upon activation of the GO signal, both devices S_1 and S_2 will be operated concurrently. Here g_1 and g_2 are the individual start signals, and d_1 and d_2 the corresponding completion signals. DONE is the overall completion signal. Figure 7.6 shows marked graph representations of the various parts of the system, including its environment. Figure 7.7 provides the behavioral specification of the system, and Fig. 7.8 shows the marked graph representation of the implementation depicted in Fig. 7.5.

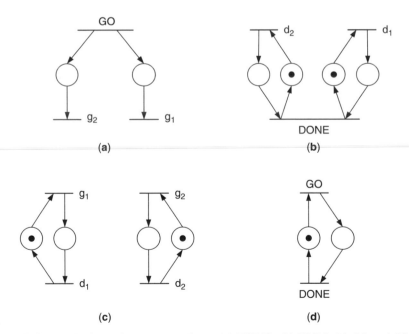

Figure 7.6   Marked graph representations: (**a**) FORK; (**b**) JOIN; (**c**) S1 and S2; (**d**) Environment of C.

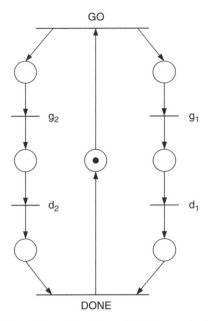

Figure 7.7   Formal specification of PS by marked graph G_{spec}.

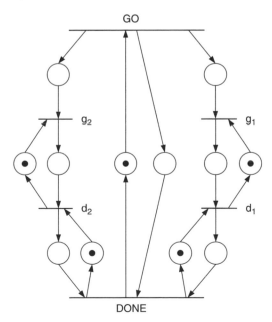

Figure 7.8   Marked graph G_{imp} representing implementation of PS.

It is easy to verify that the marked graphs of Figs 7.7 and 7.8 are L-equivalent, i.e., they determine the same language. Indeed, all marked places in Fig. 7.8, except the input place of GO, turn out to be redundant!

We will return to this example in Section 10.8.2.

7.10 FURTHER READING

For a further study of asynchronous circuits, see References 1, 3, and 5.

Reference 6 deals with decompositions of asynchronous circuits into modular networks, and their verification, using the high-level specification language LOTOS and its associated toolbox CADP, as well as Petri nets and the related tool PETRIFY.

For further insight into the relations between asynchronous circuit specifications and their implementations, see References 4, 7, and 8. These references introduce a precise formulation of the relationship between specification and realization of asynchronous circuits, and demonstrate the suitability of Petri nets and of LOTOS/CADP for the verification of modular, asynchronous circuits.

7.11 SELECTED SOLUTIONS

7.2   The relevant LOTOS file *cel.lotos* is listed in Section 7.3.1.
Apply the CADP command

$$caesar \text{ -}aldebaran \text{ } CEL.lotos$$

and then issue the command:

$$aldebaran \text{ -}omin \text{ } CEL.aut$$

The outcome is the relevant LTS:

(0,A,1)
(0,B,2)
(1,B,3)
(2,A,3)
(3,Z,0)

The relevant Petri net file *cel.net* is listed in Section 7.3.2.
Issue the command

$$write\_sg \text{ } CEL.net$$

and you will get a state graph isomorphic to the above LTS. The relevant CCS file *cel.ccs* is listed in Section 7.3.3.

Issue the command in CWB-NC:

compile cel

and you will get a suitable version of the above LTS.

7.3(a) The relevant LOTOS-file is as follows:

File ICEL.lotos
specification ICEL[A,B,Z]:noexit behaviour
    ICEL[A,B,Z]
where
  process ICEL[A,B,Z]:noexit:=
    B;Z;CEL[A,B,Z]
  endproc
  process CEL[A,B,Z]:noexit:=
    A;B;Z;CEL[A,B,Z]
    []
    B;A;Z;CEL[A,B,Z]
  endproc
endspec

_____

Now apply CADP to get the corresponding omin-file (see how in the solution to Exercise 7.2):
(0,B,1)
(1,Z,3)
(2,A,1)
(3,B,2)
(3,A,0)

_____

(b) Load the following file into your CWB-NC system:

File icel.ccs
proc icel = b.z.cel
proc cel = a.b.z.cel + b.a.z.cel

_____

Now issue the command

compile icel

You will get an LTS, strongly equivalent to the LTS listed above.

7.4   The following is a LOTOS file representing the TOGGLE module:

File tog.lotos
specification tog[a,y,z]:noexit behaviour
       tog[a,y,z]
where
  process tog[a,y,z]:noexit: =
       a;y;a;z;tog[a,y,z]
  endproc
endspec

Applying the relevant command, we get the following **tog.aut** file, as was to be expected.

File tog.aut
des(0,4,4)
(0,A,1)
(1,Y,2)
(2,A,3)
(3,Z,0)

A Petri net representation of the toggle (*tog.net*) is shown in Example 5.2 in Section 5.4. When applying the *write_sg* command to this net, we get the state graph *tog.sg* (defined there as well), which is evidently isomorphic to *tog.aut*.

7.5   The Blot representation of the CALL module can immediately be converted into a state graph *call.sg*. The essential part of call.sg is as follows:

File call.sg
s0 r1 s1
s1 r s3
s3 d s5
s5 d1 s0
s0 r2 s2
s2 r s4
s4 d s6
s6 d2 s0

Now represent *call.sg* in the appropriate PETRIFY format and then apply PETRIFY to obtain *call.net*.

7.9 Here is an efficient way of generating the file *cel3.lotos*:

File cel3.lotos
specification cel3[a,b,c,z]:noexit behaviour
     cel3[a,b,c,z]
where
  process cel3[a,b,c,z]:noexit:=
     ((a;exit ||| b;exit) ||| c;exit) >> z;cel3[a,b,c,z]
  endproc
endspec

Generating the corresponding omin-file, we get the description of a state graph with 8 states and 13 edges. An isomorphic state graph is obtained by converting the above cel3.net into a state graph.

7.13(b) Requirement (Req C1) is evidently satisfied. To verify requirement (Req C2), proceed as follows.

    Convert *XOR4.sp* and *XOR4.impl* into the corresponding LOTOS programs. Then generate the LOTOS file *XOR4ver.lotos* describing XOR4.sp || XOR4impl:

File XOR4ver.lotos
specification XOR4ver[a,b,c,d,z]:noexit behaviour
     XOR4impl[a,b,c,d,z] || XOR4sp[a,b,c,d,z]
where
  process XOR4impl[a,b,c,d,z]:noexit:=
     hide x,y in
     (XOR[a,b,x] |[x]| XOR[x,c,y]) |[y]| XOR[y,d,z]
  endproc
  process XOR4sp[a,b,c,d,z]:noexit:=
     a;z;XOR4sp[a,b,c,d,z] [] b;z;XOR4sp[a,b,c,d,z]
     [] c;z;XOR4sp[a,b,c,d,z] [] d;z;XOR4sp[a,b,c,d,z]
  endproc
  process XOR[a,b,z]:noexit:=
     a;z;XOR[a,b,z] [] b;z;XOR[a,b,z]
  endproc
endspec

Now use CADP to prove that sp || impl == sp.

Requirement (Rec C3) is best verified directly. Alternatively, you may use the −live option of Aldebaran (see Manual!).

As for requirement (Req C4), it is rather obvious that XOR4impl does not produce undesirable outputs.

7.14   First load the following two files into your CWB-NC system:

File xor4imp.ccs
proc xor1 = a.'y1.xor1 + b.'y1.xor1
proc xor2 = y1.'y2.xor2 + c.'y2.xor2
proc xor3 = y2.z.xor3 + d.z.xor3
proc xor4 = (xor1 | xor2 | xor3)\{y1,y2}

———————

File xor4sp.ccs
proc xor4sp = a.z.xor4sp + b.z.xor4sp + c.z.xor4sp + d.z.xor4sp

———————

Then issue the command

le -Smay xor4sp xor4

Recall that the above command checks for language containment. You will obtain 'TRUE'.

7.15   The following is a LOTOS file defining cel3.spec; use this file to construct the LOTOS file defining CEL3.ver:

File CEL3sp.lotos
specification CEL3SP[A,B,C,Z]:noexit behaviour
      CEL3SP[A,B,C,Z]
where
   process CEL3SP[A,B,C,Z]:noexit: =
      ((A;exit ||| B;exit) ||| C;exit) >> Z;CEL3SP[A,B,C,Z]
   endproc
endspec

———————

7.16   First load the following two files into your CWB-NC system:

File cel3sp.ccs
proc cel3sp = a.b.c.z.cel3sp + a.c.b.z.cel3sp + b.a.c.z.cel3sp +
   b.c.a.z. cel3sp + c.a.b.z.cel3sp + c.b.a.z.cel3sp

———————

File cel3imp.ccs
proc cell + a.b.'y.cell + b.a.'y.cell
proc cel2 = y.c.z.cel2 + c.y.z.cel2
proc cel3imp = (cell | cel2)\{y}

_____

Then issue the command

le -Smay cel3sp cel3imp

You will obtain 'TRUE', confirming the relevant language containment.

7.17(a) The following is a LOTOS file defining TOG3ver:

File TOG3ver.lotos
specification TOG3ver[A,W,X,Y]:noexit behaviour
    TOG3sp[A,W,X,Y] || TOG3imp[A,W,X,Y]
where
  process TOG3sp[A,W,X,Y]:noexit:=
    A;W;A;X;A;Y;TOG3sp[A,W,X,Y]
  endproc
  process TOG3imp[A,W,X,Y]:noexit:=
    hide R,S,B,Z in
    XOR[A,Z,B]|[Z,B]|(TOG[B,R,S] |[R,S]| (TOG[R,W,Y] |||
    TOG[S,X,Z]))
  endproc
  process TOG[A,Y,Z]:noexit:=
    A;Y;A;Z;TOG[A,Y,Z]
  endproc
  process XOR[A,B,Z]:noexit:=
    A;Z;XOR[A,B,Z] [] B;Z;XOR[A,B,Z]
  endproc
endspec

_____

7.17(b) The following is the PETRIFY representation of a relevant labeled net tog3lab.net:

File tog3lab.net
.model tog3lab.net
.inputs a

```
.outputs w x y
.graph
a w
w a/1
a/1 x
x a/2
a/2 y
y a
.marking { < y,a > }
.end
```

Applying the command *petrify* to this net will produce the required uniquely labeled net.

7.12 REFERENCES

1. The asynchronous logic home page. August 2006, http://intranet.cs.man.ac.uk/apt/async/.

2. Muller DE. A theory of asynchronous circuits. Technical Report 66, Digital Computer Laboratory, University of Illinois, Urbana-Champaign, December 1955.

3. Encyclopedia of delay-insensitive systems (EDIS). November 1998. http://edis.win.tue.nl/.

4. Yoeli M, Ginzburg A. LOTOS/CADP-based verification of asynchronous circuits. Computer Science Department Technical Report CS-2001-09, Technion, Israel, March 2001. Available at http://www.cs.technion.ac.il/tech-reports/.

5. Brzozowski JA, Seger C-JH. Asynchronous circuits. Springer, 1995.

6. Yoeli M. Decompositions of asynchronous circuits. Computer Science Department Technical Report CS-2001-16, Technion, Israel, April 2001. Available at http://www.cs.technion.ac.il/tech-reports/.

7. Yoeli M, Ginzburg A. Petri-net based verification of asynchronous circuits. Computer Science Department Technical Report CS0959, Technion, Israel, 1999. Available at http://www.cs.technion.ac.il/tech-reports/.

8. Yoeli M. Examples of LOTOS-based verification of asynchronous circuits. Computer Science Department Technical Report CS-2001-08, Technion, Israel, March 2001. Available at http://www.cs.technion.ac.il/tech-reports/.

## CHAPTER 8

Verification of Communication Protocols

8.1 INTRODUCTION

Communication protocols are intended to provide reliable communications over unreliable communication channels. In particular, we will be concerned with point-to-point unidirectional communication systems, transmitting messages from a *Sender* or *Transmitter* station to a *Receiver* station over an unreliable data channel. We assume that the Receiver station has facilities to confirm the receipt of a message, by sending an acknowledgement back to the Sender station over an acknowledge channel, which, in the general case, may also be unreliable.

We will assume various scenarios of possible failures, and indicate methods to overcome such failures. In particular, we are interested in verifying that the specified communication systems indeed provide reliable communication over the type of unreliable channels that we will specify in the sequel.

8.2 TWO SIMPLE COMMUNICATION PROTOCOLS

In Section 6.8.6 we introduced a very simple communication protocol (VSP), with the main purpose of illustrating the use of CCS and the associated Concurrency Workbench (CWB-NC). In this section we again use CCS and CWB-NC to present another simple communication protocol (**SCP**), which is a reduced version of the simple protocol used as the example in introducing CWB-NC (see Section 6.8). We also describe another version of this simple communication protocol (**SCP1**) based on Petri nets.

Verification of Systems and Circuits Using LOTOS, Petri Nets, and CCS, by Michael Yoeli and Rakefet Kol
Copyright © 2008 John Wiley & Sons, Inc.

8.2.1   Simple Communication Protocol SCP

To become familiar with **SCP**, enter the following files into your local C:\ directory:

File SCP.ccs
proc SE = send.'from.sack.SE
proc ME = from.'to.ME + rack.'sack.ME
proc RE = to.'rec.'rack.RE
proc PROTO = (SE | ME | RE) \ {from,to,rack,sack}

File SCP_service.ccs
proc SERVICE = send.'rec.SERVICE

The system *SCP.ccs* consists of a Sender (SE), a Receiver (RE), and a (reliable) Medium (ME). The behavior (PROTO) of the system is observation equivalent to the behavior specified by *SCP_service.ccs*.

This can be confirmed by loading the above two files into your CWB-NC system and issuing the command

eq PROTO SERVICE

The outcome is 'TRUE'.

8.2.2   Simple Communication Protocol SCP1

Using Blot, this protocol may be described as follows:

SCP1 = *[PUT;send;rec;GET;sack;rack].

EXERCISES

8.1   Transform the above description of **SCP1** into a Petri net specification using PETRIFY. Show that **SCP1** can be reduced to *[PUT;GET] by hiding all other actions.

8.2   Convert the above specification of **SCP1**, and also the specification of **SCP2** shown below, into proper LOTOS specifications. Then show that the two specifications are observation-equivalent.

$$\textbf{SCP2} := ((\textbf{cy3[PUT,send,rack]} \ ||| \ \textbf{cy3[rec,GET,sack]}) \ ||$$

$$(\textbf{cy2[send,rec]} \ ||| \ \textbf{cy2[sack,rack]})) \setminus \{\textbf{send,rec,sack,rack}\}$$

where **cy2[a,b] = a;b;cy2[a,b]** and **cy3[a,b,c] = a;b;c;cy3[a,b,c]**

8.3 THE ALTERNATING BIT (AB) PROTOCOL

8.3.1 Introduction

The Alternating Bit (AB) protocol is intended to provide a reliable data link service over a point-to-point data link with an unreliable medium.

The name of the protocol is because of the fact that the control bits 0 and 1 are alternatively appended to the messages being transmitted (over channel 1) and to the acknowledge signals (ACK), sent back (over channel 2). Both channels may be unreliable (loss of message or ACK signal, excessive delays, and so on).

Various methods have been proposed to overcome the unreliability of the channels, based on various assumptions as to the possible failures of the channels. The basic idea is that both the Transmitter (=Sender) and the Receiver will keep on sending the same message or the same ACK signal, until a clear indication is obtained from the other site that the message/ACK signal in question has indeed properly reached its destination. For an extensive discussion of the AB protocol, based on LOTOS and CADP, see Reference 1. Much of the following material is based on Reference 1.

8.3.2 The Reliable Channel Case

Here we assume that both channels (i.e., the data message channel #1 and the ACK channel #2) are completely reliable. In this case the TRANSMITTER and the RECEIVER may be specified in Blot as follows:

$$\textbf{TRANSMITTER} = \ ^*[\textbf{PUT;msg0!;ack0?;PUT;msg1!;ack1?}]$$

$$\textbf{RECEIVER} = \ ^*[\textbf{msg0?;GET;ack0!;msg1?;GET;ack1!}]$$

This is evidently a straightforward extension of the "Very Simple Protocol" (**VSP**), introduced in Section 6.8.6.

In this description we use '!' to indicate 'send' and '?' to indicate 'receive'. If we assume that only the actions 'PUT' and 'GET' are visible, the outcome of this protocol becomes

$$^*[PUT;GET]$$

In the next section we illustrate the use of Basic LOTOS to verify the above statement.

8.3.2.1 A LOTOS Description of the Reliable Channel Case
The following LOTOS specification describes the reliable channel case of the AB protocol, corresponding to its Blot description above. You should have no problems in relating the two descriptions and in following this example when attempting to "translate" Blot into proper Basic LOTOS.

File abprot1.lotos
specification abprot1[PUT,GET]:noexit behaviour
    hide msg0,msg1,ack0,ack1 in
    (
    TRANSMITTER[PUT,msg0,msg1,ack0,ack1]
    |[msg0,msg1,ack0,ack1]|
    RECEIVER[GET,msg0,msg1,ack0,ack1]
)
where
  process TRANSMITTER[PUT,msg0,msg1,ack0,ack1]:noexit:=
    PUT;   (* get next message to be sent *)
    msg0;   (* send current message + control bit 0 *)
    ack0;   (* get ack0 *)
    PUT;
    msg1;
    ack1;
    TRANSMITTER[PUT,msg0,msg1,ack0,ack1]
  endproc
  process RECEIVER[GET,msg0,msg1,ack0,ack1]:noexit:=
    msg0; (* receive message + control bit 0 *)
    GET;
    ack0; (* send ack0 *)
    msg1;
    GET;
    ack1;
    RECEIVER[GET,msg0,msg1,ack0,ack1]
  endproc
endspec

EXERCISES

8.3   We claim that this protocol reduces to just

$$^*[\mathbf{PUT;GET}]$$

provided that all other "internal" actions are hidden. To verify this claim, convert the above LOTOS file into the corresponding aut-file abprot1.aut, and then issue the command

aldebaran -omin abprot1.aut

8.4   Use CCS and CWB-NC (see Chapter 6) to verify the claim of Exercise 8.3.

8.3.3   The Unreliable Channel Case

Let us now look at a rather restricted case of unreliable channels. Assume that the TRANSMITTER sends a 1-labeled message m.1. This message becomes distorted on its way and the RECEIVER has no means to restore the original message. However, the RECEIVER has ways to discover that the message m.1 arrived distorted. Consequently, the RECEIVER sends the signal ACK.0, instead of the signal ACK.1, which would have been sent if message m.1 were to arrive without any distortion. The TRANSMITTER, upon receiving signal ACK.0, "understands" that something went wrong with message m.1 and sends message m.1 again. Similarly, we assume that the ACK-signal is never lost, but may also be distorted.

8.3.3.1 A LOTOS Verification of the Unreliable Channel Case   This case is covered in the following LOTOS file, which is a modified version of the file bitalt_protocol.lotos in Reference 1:

File abprot2.lotos
```
specification AB_PROTOCOL [PUT,GET]:noexit behaviour
hide SDT0, SDT1, RDT0, RDT1, RDTe, RACK0, RACK1, SACK0,
    SACK1, SACKe in
    (
      (
      TRANSMITTER [PUT, SDT0, SDT1, SACK0, SACK1, SACKe]
      |||
      RECEIVER [GET, RDT0, RDT1, RDTe, RACK0, RACK1]
      )
```

|[SDT0, SDT1, RDT0, RDT1, RDTe, RACK0, RACK1, SACK0, SACK1,
   SACKe]|
      (
      MEDIUM1 [SDT0, SDT1, RDT0, RDT1, RDTe]
      |||
      MEDIUM2 [RACK0, RACK1, SACK0, SACK1, SACKe]
)
)
where
   process MEDIUM1 [SDT0, SDT1, RDT0, RDT1, RDTe]:noexit :=
      SDT0;   (* send 0-message *)
      (
      RDT0;   (* transmission correct *)
         MEDIUM1 [SDT0, SDT1, RDT0, RDT1, RDTe]
      []
      RDTe;   (* message distorted *)
         MEDIUM1 [SDT0, SDT1, RDT0, RDT1, RDTe]
)
      []
      MEDIUM1 [SDT1, SDT0, RDT1, RDT0, RDTe]
   endproc
   process MEDIUM2 [RACK0, RACK1, SACK0, SACK1, SACKe]:
      noexit :=
      RACK0;   (* receiving ACK0 *)
      (
      SACK0;   (* transmission correct *)
         MEDIUM2 [RACK0, RACK1, SACK0, SACK1, SACKe]
      []
      SACKe;   (* ACK distorted *)
         MEDIUM2 [RACK0, RACK1, SACK0, SACK1, SACKe]
)
      []
      MEDIUM2 [RACK1, RACK0, SACK1, SACK0, SACKe]
   endproc
   process TRANSMITTER [PUT, SDT0, SDT1, SACK0, SACK1, SACKe]:
      noexit :=
      PUT;   (* acquiring a new message *)
         TRANSMIT [PUT, SDT0, SDT1, SACK0, SACK1, SACKe]
where
   process TRANSMIT [PUT, SDT0, SDT1, SACK0, SACK1, SACKe]:
      noexit :=
      SDT0;   (* sending a 0-message *)

```
      (
      SACK0;        (* control bit correct *)
        TRANSMITTER [PUT, SDT1, SDT0, SACK1, SACK0, SACKe]
        []
      SACK1;        (* incorrect control bit *)
          TRANSMIT [PUT, SDT0, SDT1, SACK0, SACK1, SACKe]
        []
      SACKe;        (* ACK distorted *)
          TRANSMIT [PUT, SDT0, SDT1, SACK0, SACK1, SACKe]
      )
  endproc
endproc
  process RECEIVER [GET, RDT0, RDT1, RDTe, RACK0, RACK1]:
    noexit :=
    RDT0;                 (* correct control bit *)
      GET;                (* delivery of message *)
        RACK0;            (* sending correct ACK *)
      RECEIVER [GET, RDT1, RDT0, RDTe, RACK1, RACK0]
    []
    RDT1;                 (* incorrect control bit *)
      RACK1;              (* sending incorrect ACK *)
        RECEIVER [GET, RDT0, RDT1, RDTe, RACK0, RACK1]
    []
    RDTe;                 (* message distorted *)
      RACK1;              (* sending incorrect ACK *)
        RECEIVER [GET, RDT0, RDT1, RDTe, RACK0, RACK1]
  endproc
endspec
```

EXERCISE

8.5 You should again find it easy to verify that the above protocol also reduces to

$$*[PUT;GET]$$

provided that all other actions are hidden, as indicated in the above program. However, this outcome is evidently too optimistic. It does not take into consideration the possibility that the message and/or the

ACK transmissions are always distorted! You can get a more realistic evaluation by not hiding **RDTe** and **SACKe**.

8.3.3.2 A CCS Verification of the Unreliable Channel Case   We now consider a restricted case of an unreliable medium; namely, we assume that all that may happen is the loss of messages. In particular, we illustrate the use of CCS and CWB-NC to treat this case of an unreliable medium.

The following is a CCS file covering the implementation for this case:

File abp-lossy.ccs
* Definition of Sender
proc S0 = send.S0
proc S0' = 's0.(rack0.S1 + rack1.S0' + t.S0')
proc S1 = send.S1'
proc S1' = 's1.(rack1.S0 + rack0.S1' + t.S1')
* Definition of Receiver
proc R0 = r0.'receive.'sack0.R1 + r1.'sack1.R0 + t.'sack1.R0
proc R1 = r1.'receive.'sack1.R0 + r0.'sack0.R1 + t.'sack0.R1
* Definition of the Lossy Medium "Mlossy"
proc Mlossy = s0.('r0.Mlossy + Mlossy) + s1.('r1.Mlossy + Mlossy)
    + sack0.('rack0.Mlossy + Mlossy) + sack1.('rack1.Mlossy + Mlossy)
* Internal Actions to be hidden
set Internals = {r0,r1,s0,s1,rack0,rack1,sack0,sack1}
* Definition of the Lossy Implementation "ABP-lossy"
proc ABP-lossy = (R0 | Mlossy | S0) \ Internals

The expected behavior of this implementation is formulated in the following CCS specification:

File ABPspec.ccs
proc ABPspec = send.'receive.ABPspec

We may now use CWB-NC to verify that the above implementation and specification are observational equivalent. For this purpose, we load the above two CCS files into our CWB-NC system and then issue the following command (after getting the **cwb-nc>** prompt):

eq ABPspec ABP-lossy

We get 'TRUE'.

CWB-NC also provides facilities to reduce the automaton (final-state machine) representing the above system **ABP-lossy**.

First we issue the command

size ABP-lossy

to get the relevant information:

States: 57
Transitions: 130

We may now issue the following command, to get a minimal strongly equivalent automaton:

min -S bisim ABP-lossy ABP-lossy-min

If we now issue the command

size ABP-lossy-min

we get

States: 15
Transitions: 32

Alternatively, if we issue the command

min -S obseq ABP-lossy ABP-lossy-obsmin

followed by

compile ABP-lossy-obsmin

we get the following automaton (shown in LTS format):

(0,send,1)
(1,'receive,2)
(2,send,1)
start state: 0

8.4 FURTHER READING

Presently there exists an extensive literature dealing with the verification of communication protocols. We shall point out a small selection of this literature, which we recommend for further studies.

Lai and Jirachiefpattana (2) offer a broad overview of some interesting communication protocols and their specifications and verifications. In particular, we recommend the study of the "sliding window protocol". A general introduction is presented on pp. 17–20, and a specification, using Full LOTOS, on pp. 101–105. An introduction to LOTOS, both Basic and Full, is offered on pp. 81–100. However, they do not deal with the alternating-bit protocol.

In Section 8.3.3 we demonstrated the application of Basic LOTOS to the verification of the AB protocol. However, we dealt only with part of the channel failures, discussed in Reference 1. Additional channel failures of interest, covered by Reference 1, are "total message loss" and "time-out".

While Reference 1, applying Basic LOTOS, deals only with the control part of the AB protocol, Reference 3 applies Full LOTOS, covering both the control part and the data part of the AB protocol.

For another interesting, CCS-based specification and verification of a particular version of the AB protocol, see pp. 141–149 of Robin Milner's book (4). Furthermore, the documentation for the CWB-NC (see Section 6.8) includes an exposition of the AB protocol, as a major example of a CCS-based description and verification.

Colored Petri nets have also been applied to the modeling of the AB protocol. In particular, refer to pp. 97–103 of Reference 5.

CSP (communicating sequential processes) provides another powerful approach to the modeling of the AB protocol. In particular, see Reference 6.

8.5 SELECTED SOLUTIONS

8.1 The following is the PETRIFY version describing **SCP1**:

File scp1.net
.model scp1.net
.inputs PUT
.outputs GET
.dummy send rec sack rack
.graph
#Sender
PUT send
send rac
rack PUT

#Receiver
rec GET
GET sack
sack rec
#Channels
send rec
sack rack
.marking { < rack,PUT> <sack,rec > }
.end

To reduce this net, eliminating the dummy variables, apply the command

petrify -hide.dummy scp1.net

8.4 Copy the following file **abp0.ccs** into, say, your local C:\ directory. Then load this file into your CWB-NC system and issue the command

eq ABP0 Spec

You should obtain 'TRUE'.

File abp0.ccs
* The definition of the specification "Spec"
   proc Spec = put.get.Spec
* The definition of the transmitter
   proc TR = put.msg0.'ack0.put.msg1.'ack1.TR
* The definition of the receiver
   proc RE = 'msg0.get.ack0.'msg1.get.ack1.RE
* The Internal actions to be hidden
   set Internals = {msg0,msg1,ack0,ack1}
* The definition of the implementation
   proc ABP0 = (TR|RE) \ Internals

8.6 REFERENCES

1. Alternating bit without data part, demo_01 from CADP on-line demo examples, 2006. http://www.inrialpes.fr/vasy/cadp/demos.html.

2. Lai R, Jirachiefpattana A. Communication protocol specification and verification. Kluwer, 1998.
3. Alternating bit with data part, demo_02 from CADP on-line demo examples, 2006. http://www.inrialpes.fr/vasy/cadp/demos.html.
4. Milner R. Communication and concurrency. Prentice-Hall, 1989.
5. Girault C, Valk R. Petri nets for systems engineering. Springer, 2003.
6. Roscoe AW. The theory and practice of concurrency. Prentice-Hall, 1998.

## CHAPTER 9

Verification of Arbiters

9.1 INTRODUCTION

An arbiter circuit controls the exclusive access of one out of a number of possibly competing processes to a shared resource.

There are a number of possible algorithms for choosing the process that gets access to the resource in case of two or more competing processes. Here we only list a few examples and in Section 9.5 we provide relevant references for further study:

- random arbiter—the selection is done at random
- token-ring arbiter—the selection is done in a fixed cyclic order
- priority arbiter—the selection is done according to fixed or changing priorities assigned to the processes in question

We expect an arbiter circuit to satisfy the following requirements:

(1) **Mutual Exclusion:** only one process may have access to the shared resource
(2) **Grant Only on Request**
(3) **Fairness:** any request by a process is eventually granted

9.2 A RANDOM ARBITER (RGDA)

We consider a circuit that has one binary incoming line INj from each process $\#j$, and one binary outgoing line $OUTj$ to each process $\#j$, as described in Fig. 9.1. The rising-transition of INj is denoted Rj (request), its falling-transition is denoted Dj (done). Similarly, the rise- and fall-transitions of

Verification of Systems and Circuits Using LOTOS, Petri Nets, and CCS, by
Michael Yoeli and Rakefet Kol
Copyright © 2008 John Wiley & Sons, Inc.

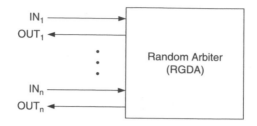

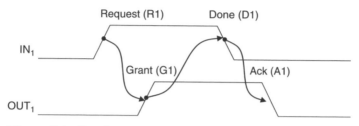

Figure 9.1   Random RGDA arbiter interfaces and waveforms.

OUT*j* are denoted G*j* (grant) and A*j* (acknowledge), respectively. The various line changes (as can be seen in Fig. 9.1) are interpreted as follows:

(1) R1: process #1 requests access (to the shared resource)
(2) G1: the resource is free and access is granted
(3) D1: process #1 releases the resource
(4) A1: access withdrawn

We will refer to such an arbiter as an RGDA arbiter, based on these four phases of its operation (Request, Grant, Done, and Acknowledge).
We shall now consider a two-processes random arbiter as specified above.

9.2.1   Verifying RGDA Using LOTOS

9.2.1.1   *Blot and LOTOS Representation of RGDA*   The Blot representation of the RGDA is given by

RGDA.blot =
$$*[R1;G1;D1;A1] \parallel$$
$$*[R2;G2;D2;A2] \parallel$$
$$*[G1;D1 [ ] G2;D2]$$

The first two lines represent the cyclic behavior of the two processes and the last line is a way to specify the mutual exclusion requirement. For a similar representation, see Reference 1.

Now try to convert the above Blot representation into a proper LOTOS representation, before you continue reading! You should come up with something similar to the following:

File arb1.lotos
specification arb1[R1,G1,D1,A1,R2,G2,D2,A2]:noexit behaviour
      (cy[R1,G1,D1,A1] ||| cy[R2,G2,D2,A2]) |[G1,D1,G2,D2]|
         mex[G1,D1,G2,D2]
where
   process cy[R,G,D,A]:noexit:=
     R;G;D;A;cy[R,G,D,A]
   endproc
   process mex[G1,D1,G2,D2]:noexit:=
     G1;D1;mex[G1,D1,G2,D2]
     []
     G2;D2;mex[G1,D1,G2,D2]
   endproc
endspec

Now convert the above LOTOS file into the corresponding aut-file, and then issue the command:

aldebaran -omin arb1.aut > arb1.omin

Here, arb1.omin is a state-graph representation of the RGDA arbiter, equivalent to the one shown in Fig. 9.2.

9.2.1.2 *Verification of RGDA Using LOTOS* Let us now check whether the requirements formulated in Section 9.1 are indeed satisfied. Here we combine the use of Blot and Basic LOTOS.

9.2.1.2.1 Verifying Mutual Exclusion One way of showing that the mutual exclusion requirement is indeed satisfied is as follows. We consider **arb_red1 = arb\{R1,R2,A1,A2}** and then minimize the outcome. The Blot representation of the result will be *[G1;D1 [] G2;D2]. The following is a LOTOS file representing arb_red1, obtained by an evident reduction of the

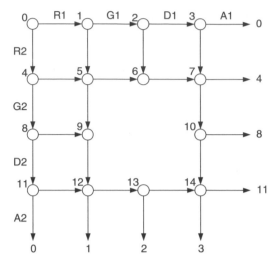

Figure 9.2 State-graph representation of the RGDA arbiter.

original file *arb1.lotos* described above (a more formal reduction can be obtained by using the **hide** facility of Basic LOTOS):

File arb_red1.lotos
specification arb_red1[G1,D1,G2,D2]:noexit behaviour
      (cy2[G1,D1] ||| cy2[G2,D2]) || mex[G1,D1,G2,D2]
where
   process cy2[G1,D1]:noexit:=
      G1;D1;cy2[G1,D1]
   endproc
   process mex[G1,D1,G2,D2]:noexit:=
      G1;D1;mex[G1,D1,G2,D2]
      []
      G2;D2;mex[G1,D1,G2,D2]
   endproc
endspec

EXERCISE

9.1 Use the **hide** facility of CADP to achieve the preceding reduction of arb1.lotos. Use CADP to compare the outcomes of the two reduction approaches.

9.2.1.2.2 Verifying Grant Only on Request In order to verify this requirement, we hide the D's and A's in arb1.lotos. This will show that R1 and G1 alternate, and so do R2 and G2.

9.2.1.2.3 Verifying Fairness The above arbiter is not fair! Namely process #1 may hold on to the resource forever, although process #2 has requested it. Indeed, the following infinite event sequence is feasible:

$$R1;G1;R2;D1;A1;(R1;G1;D1;A1;)\infty$$

where ∞ denotes "repeat forever."

9.2.2 Verifying RGDA Using Petri Nets

9.2.2.1 Petri Net Representation of RGDA As indicated previously, it is quite easy to convert a Blot expression into a corresponding Petri net. The following is a PETRIFY description of a net corresponding to the above Blot representation *RGDA.blot*:

File arb1.net
```
.model arb1.net
.inputs R1 R2 D1 D2
.outputs G1 G2 A1 A2
.graph
#process #1
R1 G1
G1 D1
D1 A1
A1 R1
#process #2
R2 G2
G2 D2
D2 A2
A2 R2
#mutual exclusion
p0 G1 G2
A1 p0
A2 p0
.marking {<A1,R1> <A2,R2> p0}
.cnd
```

To view a graphical representation of the above net *arb1.net*, you may proceed as follows.

Issue the command

$$draw\_astg\ arb1.net > arb1.ps$$

Then apply the **ghostview** command to *arb1.ps* to see the net (cf. Fig. 9.3).

9.2.2.2 Verification of RGDA Using Petri Net

9.2.2.2.1 Verifying Mutual Exclusion We have to show that event G1 ("the resource is granted to process #1") may be followed by event G2 only if event D1 ("resource released by process #1") intervenes. Similarly, D2 must intervene, should G2 be followed by G1.

One way of verifying this requirement is to "hide" (i.e., replace by λ) events R1, R2, A1, and A2, in *arb1.net*. The algebraic representation of the outcome (after omitting λ-events) becomes

> *[G1;D1] ‖
> *[G2;D2] ‖
> *[G1;D1 [] G2;D2]

It is easily verified that this expression reduces to *[G1;D1 [] G2;D2]. This reduced algebraic expression evidently verifies the mutual exclusion requirement.

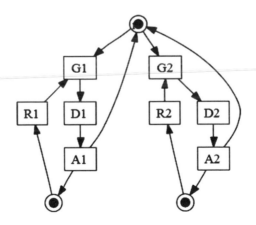

INPUTS: R1,R2,D1,D2
OUTPUTS: G1,G2,A1,A2

Figure 9.3 Petri net graphical representation of the RGDA arbiter.

Another method is the following. Consider the token count of the circuit

<G1,D1>, <D1,A1>, <A1,G2>, <G2,D2>, <D2,A2>, <A2,G1>

It is easy to verify that this token count is constantly 1. Namely, the token count is initially 1, and is not changed by the firing of any transition. This fact ensures that the mutual exclusion requirement is indeed met.

EXERCISE

9.2 In the above PETRIFY representation of arb1.net declare R1, R2, A1, A2 as "dummy". Then apply the command

petrify -hide .dummy arb1.net

and prove that the outcome is equivalent to *[G1;D1 [] G2;D2].

9.2.2.2.2 Verifying Grant Only on Request In order to verify the grant only on request requirement, we may proceed similarly to what we did in Section 9.2.1 by hiding the D's and A's.

9.2.2.2.3 Verifying Fairness The same reasons described in Section 9.2.1 also apply, of course, for this representation. Hence the above arbiter is not fair.

9.2.3 Verifying RGDA Using CCS

The description in CCS of a simple RGDA arbiter between two processes is given by the following file:

File arb.ccs
proc arb = req1.grant1.done1.ack1.arb + req2.grant2.done2.ack2.arb

————————

To check for the Mutual Exclusion property with the CWB-NC tool, we define the following two optional description files in mu-calculus format and CTL format:

File mutex_mu.mu
prop mutex = max X = ([grant1]ff ∨ [grant2]ff) ∧ [-]X

————————

File mutex_ctl.mu
prop mutex1 = AG ([grant1]ff $\lor$ [grant2]ff)

———————

Now issue the following commands to verify the property:

chk arb mutex_mu

chk arb mutex_ctl

As expected, the result in both cases is 'TRUE'.

We now turn to the application of CCS to the specification and verification of the original RGDA arbiter, as introduced in Section 9.2.1 (see also Fig. 9.2). For this purpose, we construct the following files *rgda1.ccs* and *rgda1.mu*:

File rgda1.ccs
proc Q0 = r1.Q1 + r2.Q4
proc Q1 = g1.Q2 + r2.Q5
proc Q2 = d1.Q3 + r2.Q6
proc Q3 = a1.Q0 + r2.Q7
proc Q4 = r1.Q5 + g2.Q8
proc Q5 = g1.Q6 + g2.Q9
proc Q6 = d1.Q7
proc Q7 = a1.Q4 + g2.Q10
proc Q8 = r1.Q9 + d2.Q11
proc Q9 = d2.Q12
proc Q10 = a1.Q8 + d2.Q14
proc Q11 = r1.Q12 + a2.Q0
proc Q12 = g1.Q13 + a2.Q1
proc Q13 = d1.Q14 + a2.Q2
proc Q14 = a1.Q11 + a2.Q3

———————

The above CCS file is evidently isomorphic to Fig. 9.2. Note that the initial state of this CCS file is Q0.

The following file lists some required properties, in CTL formulation:

File rgda1.mu
prop mutex = AG([d1]ff $\lor$ [d2]ff)
prop evg = EF[g1]tt $\land$ EF[g2]tt
prop dlf1 = AG<->tt

———————

You may now use your CWB-NC system to verify the above properties. After loading both files into your CWB-NC system, issue, e.g., the command

chk Q0 mutex

to confirm the first of the above three properties.

For additional CCS analysis of other arbiters, see Reference 2.

9.3 A TOKEN-RING ARBITER

In this section we specify a distributed arbiter serving three processes. The extension to $n > 3$ processes is evident. We specify the arbiter considered by a Petri net with a constant token count of 1. Thus mutual exclusion is assured. The net contains a cycle ("ring") formed by places p0, p1, p2. If the token is in one of these places, the corresponding process (#1,#2,#3) has access to the shared resource.

9.3.1 A Petri Net Representation of a Token-Ring Arbiter

Using PETRIFY, the arbiter in question may be specified as follows:

File torarb3.net
```
.model torarb3.net
.inputs R1 R2 R3 D1 D2 D3
.outputs G1 G2 G3 A1 A2 A3
.internal  X1 X2 X3
.graph
# process #1
p0 R1
R1 G1
G1 D1
D1 A1
A1 p1
# process #2
p1 R2
R2 G2
G2 D2
D2 A2
A2 p2
# process #3
p2 R3
R3 G3
```

```
G3 D3
D3 A3
A3 p0
# token ring
p0 X1
X1 p1
p1 X2
X2 p2
p2 X3
X3 p0
.marking {p0}
.end
```

9.3.2   Verification of a Token-Ring Arbiter Using Petri Net

As mentioned above, the token count in this net is constantly 1, ensuring mutual exclusion.

It is easy to verify that each process will eventually gain access to the shared resource. And since Gi always follows Ri, a grant output must follow the relevant request input.

In order to provide fairness, we must postulate that input transitions have priority over internal transitions.

EXERCISES

9.1   Extend the RGDA arbiter to three competing processes. Verify this arbiter similarly to

(**a**) Section 9.2.1 for a LOTOS representation

(**b**) Section 9.2.2 for a Petri net representation

9.2   Extend the RGDA arbiter to one where three processes share two copies of a common resource. Specify and verify this arbiter using a Petri net, similar to what we did in Section 9.2.2.

9.4   FURTHER READING

An extensive literature is available dealing with the specification and verification of a variety of arbiter designs. Many of them apply tools that are beyond the scope of this text. Here we present a selection of interesting approaches, together with their documentation.

Regarding priority arbiters, see Reference 3.

Token-ring arbiters are handled by References 4–6.

For information on tree arbiters, see References 7 and 8.

9.5 SELECTED SOLUTIONS

9.1 Replace the first line of *arb1.lotos* by

> specification arb_red2[G1,D1,G2,D2]:noexit behaviour
>   hide R1,A1,R2,A2 in

Then confirm that *arb_red2.aut* and *arb_red1.aut* are observation-equivalent, but are not strongly equivalent.

9.2 Change the file *arb1.net* into file *arb1_red1.net* by proceeding as follows. Replace the first three lines of the file *arb1.net* by the following four lines:

```
.model arb1_red1.net
.inputs D1 D2
.outputs G1 G2
.dummy R1 R2 A1 A2
```

Then issue the command

> ***petrify -hide .dummy arb1_red1.net***.

The outcome is evidently isomorphic to *[G1;D1 [] G2;D2].

9.3 The relevant Blot specification is as follows:

```
RGDA3.blot =
    *[R1;G1;D1;A1]  ||
    *[R2;G2;D2;A2]  ||
    *[R3;G3;D3;A3]  ||
    *[G1;D1 [] G2;D2 [] G3;D3]
```

Transform this Blot spec into the corresponding LOTOS file and then proceed as in Section 9.2.1.

9.4 The relevant net *3arb.net* is as follows (in PETRIFY syntax representation):

File 3arb.net
.model 3arb.net

```
.inputs R1 R2 R3 D1 D2 D3
.outputs G1 G2 G3 A1 A2 A3
graph
#process #1
R1 G1
G1 D1
D1 A1
A1 R1
#process #2
R2 G2
G2 D2
D2 A2
A2 R2
#process #3
R3 G3
G3 D3
D3 A3
A3 R3
#mutual exclusion
p0 G1 G2 G3
A1 p0
A2 p0
A3 p0
.capacity p0 = 2
.marking {<A1,R1> <A2,R2> <A3,R3> p0 = 2}
.end
```

Verification

Mutual Exclusion

First, consider the token count of the following circuits:

$$[Ri, Gi, Di, Ai, Ri]$$

This token count is evidently constant, equaling 1. Thus we can have only one token in the "critical" section $[Gi, Di, Ai]$. On the other hand, consider the token count of the following subnet:

```
p0 G1 G2 G3
G1 D1
D1 A1
```

```
A1 p0
G2 D2
D2 A2
A2 p0
G3 D3
D3 A3
A3 p0
```

It is easily verified that the token count of this subnet equals constantly 2. Hence no more than two processes are enabled at any time.

Grant Only on Request
The method of verification used in Section 9.2.2 is evidently applicable.

Fairness
Fairness is not assured! Indeed, e.g., process #1 together with process #2 may prevent process #3 from accessing either of the two resources.

9.6   REFERENCES

1. RGDA Arbiter. From the Encyclopedia of Delay-Insensitive Systems (EDIS), November 1998. http://edis.win.tue.nl/sys/rgda-arbiter/.
2. Bruns G. Distributed systems analysis with CCS. Prentice-Hall, 1997.
3. Bystrov A, Kinniment DJ, Yakovlev A. Priority arbiters. Department of Computer Science, University of Newcastle-upon-Tyne, UK. TR-CS-687, October 1999.
4. Martin A. Distributed mutual exclusion on a ring of processes. Sci. Comp. Programming 1985;5:265–276.
5. Ebergen JC. Arbiters Sci Comp Programming 1992;18:223–245.
6. Low KS, Yakovlev A. Token ring arbiters. Department of Computer Science, University of Newcastle-upon-Tyne, UK. TR-CS-537, November 1995.
7. Mitrani I, Yakovlev A. Tree arbiters with nearest neighbour scheduling. In: Proceedings of 13th International Symposium on Computer and Information Science, October 1998, Belek, Turkey.
8. Genrich HJ, Shapiro RM. Formal verification of an arbiter cascade. Lecture Notes in Computer Science 1992;616:205–223.

## CHAPTER 10

More Verification Case Studies

In this chapter we discuss some additional verification case studies, further illustrating the application of the major tools discussed in Chapters 4–6.

10.1 VERIFICATION OF COMBINATIONAL LOGIC

As indicated in Chapter 1, the major part of this book deals with the event-based approach to the specification, description, and verification of circuits and systems. However, we also devote a small part of this text to the level-based approach, particularly in connection with the use of Full LOTOS (see Section 4.9).

Indeed, in Section 4.9.1 we illustrated the application of Full LOTOS to the description of the NOT-gate, using a level-based approach. In this section we continue our use of Full LOTOS to the level-based descriptions of two-input combinational gates.

10.1.1 The AND Gate

We start with the AND-gate. This gate has two inputs, say in1 and in2. When stable, the output becomes out $=$ in1 $\wedge$ in2. The AND operator $\wedge$ is referred to in the library 'BOOLEAN' (see Section 4.9) as 'and'.

The following is one way of specifying a (non-terminating) two-input AND-gate using Full LOTOS:

File ANDgate.lotos
specification ANDgate[in1,in2,out]:noexit
library BOOLEAN endlib
behaviour
        ANDgate[in1,in2,out]

Verification of Systems and Circuits Using LOTOS, Petri Nets, and CCS, by Michael Yoeli and Rakefet Kol
Copyright © 2008 John Wiley & Sons, Inc.

where
    process ANDgate[in1,in2,out]:noexit:=
        (in1 ?x:Bool;
        in2 ?y:Bool;
        out! (x and y);
        ANDgate[in1,in2,out])
        []
        (in2 ?y:Bool;
        in1 ?x:Bool;
        out! (y and x);
        ANDgate[in1,in2,out])
    endproc
endspec

In this version of the AND-gate, the two gate inputs are assumed to appear sequentially, one after the other. Therefore the following two possibilities are considered: either in1 appears first or in2 appears first.

Proceeding similarly to Section 4.9.1.2, we may use CADP to derive the file *ANDgate.aut*. Namely, we first issue the command

caesar.adt ANDgate.lotos

followed by

caesar -aldebaran ANDgate.lotos

However, there is a point in simplifying the file *ANDgate.aut* obtained, by applying the command

aldebaran -omin ANDgate.aut

producing the following *ANDgate.omin* file:

File ANDgate.omin
des (0, 14, 7)
(0, "IN1 !FALSE", 6)
(0, "IN1 !TRUE", 3)
(0, "IN2 !FALSE", 5)
(0, "IN2 !TRUE", 1)
(1, "IN1 !FALSE", 2)
(1, "IN1 !TRUE", 4)
(2, "OUT !FALSE", 0)

(3, "IN2 !FALSE", 2)
(3, "IN2 !TRUE", 4)
(4, "OUT !TRUE", 0)
(5, "IN1 !FALSE", 2)
(5, "IN1 !TRUE", 2)
(6, "IN2 !FALSE", 2)
(6, "IN2 !TRUE", 2)

In the file *ANDgate.lotos* shown above it was assumed that the two inputs are read sequentially, in any order. Alternatively, we may assume that the two inputs are read in parallel. The corresponding LOTOS file *ANDgate1.lotos* is as follows; you may consider this file as the standard way to represent two inputs appearing in parallel at a gate:

File ANDgate1.lotos
specification ANDgate1[IN1,IN2,OUT]:noexit
library BOOLEAN endlib
behaviour
       ANDgate1[IN1,IN2,OUT]
where
   process ANDgate1[IN1,IN2,OUT]:noexit :=
      (IN1 ?x:Bool;exit(x, any Bool)
      |||
      IN2 ?y:Bool;exit(any Bool,y))
      >>
      accept x,y: Bool in OUT!(x and y);
      ANDgate1[IN1,IN2,OUT]
   endproc
endspec

The corresponding omin-file *ANDgate1.omin* coincides essentially with the file *ANDgate.omin*, except for a different labeling of the graph nodes.

10.1.2 Composite Gates

Other 2-input gates, such as OR-, XOR-, and EQUALITY-gates, may be handled very similarly to the above way of dealing with AND-gates. In this section we show how gates can be interconnected to generate composite gates, somewhat similar to the way composite modules may be formed by interconnecting basic modules.

As an example, we will take a NAND-gate. Recall the definition of the logical nand-operator; namely, x nand y = ~(x and y). Accordingly, a NAND-gate may be constructed by the interconnection of an AND-gate and a NOT-gate. Such a construction is implemented in the following file:

File NAND1.lotos
```
specification NAND1[in1,in2,out]:noexit
library BOOLEAN endlib
behaviour
        NAND1[in1,in2,out]
where
   process NAND1[in1,in2,out]:noexit:=
        NAND[in1,in2,out]>>NAND1[in1,in2,out]
   endproc
   process NAND[in1,in2,out]:exit:=
        hide out1 in
        (AND[in1,in2,out1] |[out1]| NOT0[out1,out])
   endproc
   process NOT0 [IN1, OUT]:exit:=
        IN1 ?x:Bool;
        OUT! not(x);
        exit
   endproc
   process AND [IN1,IN2,OUT]:exit:=
        (IN1 ?x:Bool;exit(x,any Bool)
        |||
        IN2 ?y:Bool;exit(any Bool,y))
        >>
        accept x,y:Bool in  (OUT! (x and y); exit)
   endproc
endspec
```

In gate compositions, such as the above, we first construct the non-recursive part of the composite gate, using non-recursive versions of the participating components. We then add recursion, as illustrated in the example above.

Using CADP, we may process the above file *NAND1.lotos*, as explained in Section 10.1.1, to derive the corresponding file *NAND1.omin*. This file can be obtained immediately from the above file *ANDgate.omin*, by replacing "OUT! TRUE" with "OUT! FALSE", and vice versa.

EXERCISES

10.1 Design a file *NAND2.lotos*, similar to the file *ANDgate1*. The essential difference is the replacement of (x and y) by not(x and y). Generate the relevant aut-file and show that this file is observation-equivalent to the aut-file derived from the above file NAND1.lotos.

10.2 Recall that $x \wedge y = \sim(\sim x \vee \sim y)$. Design a composite gate corresponding to the right-hand side of this equation. Derive the corresponding aut-file and show that this file is observation equivalent to the aut-file derived from *ANDgate.lotos*.

10.3 Design level-based specifications of a three-input XOR-gate as follows:

(a) File *XOR3comp.lotos* specifying the interconnection of two XOR-gates.

(b) File *XOR3gate.lotos*, using a three-input Boolean xor-component. Show that the two designs are observation-equivalent.

10.2 VERIFICATION OF ASYNCHRONOUS PIPELINE CONTROLLERS

10.2.1 Introduction

A useful mechanism for increasing the speed at which data processing units cooperate is the *pipeline*. Consider a sequence of data processing operations, which are conveniently decomposed into two parts. The first part is processed by data processing unit A, and the following part is processed by unit B. By connecting unit A to unit B via a pipeline, both units may operate concurrently. Unit A deposits any processed part into the pipeline, and it is extracted from the pipeline by unit B for further processing. Thus such a pipeline essentially serves as a FIFO (First-In, First-Out) queue. The pipeline consists of a sequence of *stages*, through which each data part is passed, stage by stage, from A to B. At each stage the data are stored in a set of latches.

In this section we consider relevant latch control units (LCUs), operating asynchronously (no clock involved). We follow to a large extent the well-known Turing award paper by Sutherland (1), who refers to the corresponding pipeline as *micropipeline*.

A diagram of a typical micropipeline is shown in Fig. 10.1.

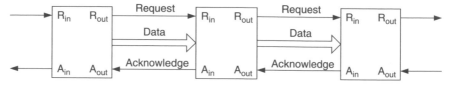

Figure 10.1   Micropipeline.

10.2.1.1 *Transition Signaling*   A Latch Control Unit (LCU) is preferably viewed as event-based, rather than level-based. In particular, both up-transitions and down-transitions are meaningful signals. Such a signaling scheme is referred to as *transition signaling* or *2-phase signaling*. An alternative signaling scheme is the *4-phase* signaling, in which only up-transitions are meaningful signals, and the down-transitions serve to return the circuit to its initial condition.

10.2.1.2 *The Bundled Data Interface*   There are various ways in which a Sender may transfer data to a Receiver asynchronously (i.e., no synchronizing clock is involved). The method discussed in Reference 1 is referred to as *bundled data interface protocol*, and is illustrated in Fig. 10.2.

The data wires carry conventional logic level signals, i.e., high or low. When the Sender wishes to send data to the Receiver, it places the data on the Data wires, and initiates a transition (up or down) on the Request wire. Upon receipt of this transition, the Receiver stores the data sent in a set of latches and initiates a transition on the Acknowledge wire.

In this scheme it is essential that the data reach the Receiver before the Request signal does!

10.2.2 Latch Control Unit

10.2.2.1 *A Blot Specification of LCU*   A Latch Control Unit (LCU) has IN-connections RIN? and AIN! and OUT-connections ROUT! and AOUT? ('?' denotes input and '!' denotes output).

Figure 10.2   Bundled data interface.

The outside connections of an LCU (see Fig. 10.1) may be interpreted as follows:

- RIN? indicates that data are ready to enter the LCU.
- AIN! confirms that the relevant data have been stored in a set of latches.
- ROUT! indicates that the relevant data are available for the following LCU. Note that ROUT! is connected to RIN? of the following LCU.
- AOUT? is connected to AIN! of the following LCU.

The IN-connections always alternate, and so do the OUT-connections. Following Reference 1, we assume that the two sides are connected by the alternation of AIN! and ROUT!.

Using Blot, the above LCU may be specified as follows:

LCUspec = *[RIN;AIN] || *[AIN;ROUT] || *[ROUT;AOUT]

The implementation may be represented by

LCUimp = ICEL[ROUT, RIN, AIN] || ICEL[AOUT, AIN, ROUT]

In view of the example in Section 7.7.2, it becomes evident that **LCUimp** is a Type-A1 realization of **LCUspec**.

10.2.2.2 A LOTOS Specification of LCU   The LOTOS file representing the specification of a latch control unit is as follows:

File LCUspec.lotos
specification LCUspec[RIN,AIN,ROUT,AOUT]:noexit behaviour
    (CY2[RIN,AIN]|||CY2[ROUT,AOUT]) |[AIN,ROUT]| CY2[AIN,ROUT]
where
    process CY2[A,B]:noexit:=
        A;B;CY2[A,B]
    endproc
endspec

Here CY2[A,B] evidently means that A and B alternate.

10.2.2.3 A LOTOS Implementation of LCU   The corresponding implementation (see Reference 1) is represented by the following:

File LCUimp.lotos
specification LCUimp[RIN,AIN,ROUT,AOUT]:noexit behaviour
        ICEL[ROUT,RIN,AIN] |[AIN,ROUT]| ICEL[AOUT,AIN,ROUT]

where
  process ICEL[A,B,Z]:noexit:=
     B;Z;CEL[A,B,Z]
  endproc
  process CEL[A,B,Z]:noexit:=
     A;B;Z;CEL[A,B,Z]
     []
     B;A;Z;CEL[A,B,Z]
  endproc
endspec

It is interesting to observe that the latch control unit specified above is isomorphic to an up–down transition counter with the range 0–3, provided that events are suitably relabeled. We shall discuss transition counters in Section 10.5.

EXERCISES

10.4(a)   Use Blot to prove directly that *LCUimp.lotos* and *LCUspec.lotos* are strongly equivalent.
  (b)   Use CADP to produce the above proof.

10.5   Let 2LCUsp = *[rin;ain] ‖ *[ain;rint] ‖ *[rint;aint] ‖ *[aint;rout] ‖ *[rout;aout].
  (a)   Design a suitable implementation of 2LCUsp.
  (b)   Verify this implementation directly (using Blot).

10.2.2.4 Latch Problems   Conventional latches are level-controlled and not event-controlled. Thus a problem evidently arises when an event-controlled LCU is to be connected to a level-controlled latch. Sutherland (1) introduced a specially designed event-controlled latch to deal with this problem. However, other researchers prefer to use conventional latches, applying both 2-phase as well as 4-phase signaling. In such systems, methods of phase conversion are of importance. We discuss various such conversion methods in the next section.

A variety of micropipeline designs, dealing with various aspects of the above problem, as well as with related problems, have been proposed. For more information, see, e.g., References 2–6.

10.2.3   Phase Converters

10.2.3.1   2-Phase to 4-Phase Converter (PC24)   Let [b;y] be the
signaling sequence used in 2-phase signaling, where b is the Request signal
and y is the Acknowledge signal. Let [a;z;a;z] be the corresponding
4-phase signaling sequence. A PC24 has the connections shown in
Fig. 10.3 and is specified by the following Blot expression:

$$PC24 = *[b;a;z;a;z;y]$$

Let us now look at a Type-C realization (see Section 7.7.4) as an
implementation of the above specification. Following the converters section
in Reference 7, the realization in question can be represented by the following
Blot expression:

$$PC24.imp = (XOR[b,x,a] \parallel TOG[z,x,y]) \backslash \{x\}$$

For a direct verification of the Type-C realization, and in order to verify
requirement (Req C2) of Section 7.9.4, we consider the Blot expression

$$PC24VER := XOR[b,x,a] \parallel TOG[z,x,y] \parallel *[b;a;z;a;z;y]$$

We wish to show that

$$PC24VER \backslash \{x\} == PC24$$

It is easy to verify that PC24VER is capable of performing only the following sequence of actions:

$$PC24VER \ [b;a;z;x;a;z;y > PC24VER$$

Thus we indeed have PC24VER\\{x} ==PC24.
We now turn to a CADP-based verification of PC24. To verify that
PC24.imp is indeed a Type-C realization of PC24, we convert the two Blot
expressions into proper LOTOS files (*PC24imp.lotos* and *PC24sp.lotos*) and
proceed similarly to the examples in Chapter 7.

Figure 10.3   2-Phase to 4-phase converter (PC24) interfaces.

For the complete LOTOS-based verification, see Exercise 10.6 below.
For a CCS-based verification of PC24, consider the following files:

File pc24spec.ccs
proc pc24spec = b.a.z.a.z.y.pc24spec

File pc24imp.ccs
proc comp1 = b.a.comp1+'x.a.comp1
proc comp2 = z.x.z.y.comp2
proc pc24imp = (comp1|comp2)\{x}

We wish to show that L(pc24spec) is a subset of L(pc24imp). This we
achieve by loading the above two files into our CWB-NC system, and
issuing the command

le -Smay pc24spec pc24imp

The outcome is 'TRUE', confirming the above statement.

EXERCISE

10.6 Provide the details of the above CADP-based verification.

10.2.3.2 4-Phase to 2-Phase Converter (PC42) This type of converter handles the conversion of a 4-phase sequence [a;z;a;z] into a 2-phase
sequence [b;y].
A typical Blot specification is

$$PC42spec = *[a;b;z;(a;\$ ||| y;\$) >> z;\$]$$

This specification may be realized by the following implementation in
Blot:

$$PC42imp = (TOG[a,b,x1] || (CEL[x1,y,x2] || XOR[b,x2,z])\setminus\{x1,x2\}$$

EXERCISE

10.7 Prove that **PC42imp** is indeed a Type-C realization of **PC42spec**.

10.3 VERIFICATION OF PRODUCER–CONSUMER SYSTEMS

10.3.1 Introduction

The "producer–consumer problem" plays an important role in most operating systems. A particular system that we are interested in consists of a *producer*, a *bounded buffer*, and a *consumer*. The producer produces new items (typically data) intended to be used (consumed) by the consumer. The items are transferred via the bounded buffer. If this buffer is full, then the producer has to wait (to prevent "overflow"). If the buffer is empty, then the consumer has to wait.

10.3.2 Verifying Producer–Consumer Systems Using Petri Nets

The PETRIFY file *pc.net* shown below describes a particular producer–consumer system, with buffer capacity of $n = 3$. The actions involved are

- prod: produce a new item
- dep: deposit an item into the buffer
- take: take an item from the buffer
- cons: consume the item

File pc.net
```
.inputs prod dep take cons
.graph
# the producer
p1 prod
prod p2
p2 dep
dep p1
# the consumer
p3 take
take p4
p4 cons
cons p3
# the buffer
dep p5
p5 take
take p6
p6 dep
```

.capacity p5 = 3 p6 = 3
.marking {p1 p3 p6 = 3}
.end

Note that the marking of p6 indicates the number of free buffer positions, and the marking of p5 indicates the number of occupied buffer positions.

10.3.3 Occurrence Counts

For verification of the above producer–consumer system, we first need to introduce the concept of "occurrence counts". Occurrence counts, as described below, provide yet another useful tool for the verification of certain properties of Petri nets.

Let $PN = (P,T,F,M0)$ be a Petri net, as defined in 5.1.3. For any node x in $(P \cup T)$ we denote by $\bullet x$ the set of input nodes of x and by $x \bullet$ its set of output nodes. Let σ be an occurrence sequence of PN and let S be a subset of T. We denote by $\#(\sigma,S)$ the "S-count" of σ, i.e., the number of occurrences of S-elements in σ. If S is a singleton, i.e., $S = \{t\}$, we write $\#(\sigma,t)$ instead of $\#(\sigma,\{t\})$. Now let p be a place of PN, and let M be a marking of PN reachable by applying the occurrence sequence σ to M0. We evidently have

$$M(p) = M0(p) + \#(\sigma,\bullet p) - \#(\sigma,p\bullet).$$

Namely, every input transition of p, when fired, increases the token count of p by 1, and every output transition of p, when fired, decreases the token count of p by 1. In particular, since always $M(p) \geq 0$, every occurrence sequence σ of PN must satisfy the following occurrence count condition for every place p of PN:

$$M0(p) + \#(\sigma,\bullet p) - \#(\sigma,p\bullet) \geq 0.$$

10.3.4 Verifying the Producer–Consumer System Using Occurrence Counts

10.3.4.1 Verifying Liveness   We start by proving the liveness of the system. Note that *pc.net* (from Section 10.3.2) is a marked graph. To prove its liveness, we show that every simple directed circuit has positive token count. By inspection, we recognize the three simple directed circuits $C1 = \{p1,p2\}$, $C2 = \{p3,p4\}$, and $C3 = \{p5,p6\}$. The token counts of both C1 and C2 are one and the token count of C3 is $n > 0$. Thus the net is live.

10.3.4.2 Verifying Boundedness Since both circuits C1 and C2 have a constant token count of 1, it follows that places p1, p2, p3, p4 are safe. Furthermore, since C3 has a constant token count of $n > 0$, places p5 and p6 are bounded by n.

10.3.4.3 Verifying Overflow/Underflow Let σ be an arbitrary occurrence sequence of the net in question (*pc.net*). Let $d = \#(\sigma,\text{dep}) - \#(\sigma,\text{take})$. Since the buffer capacity is assumed to be n, "buffer overflow" will occur whenever $d > n$. A "buffer underflow" will occur whenever $d < 0$, i.e., the number of "take" attempts exceeds the number of deposits.

To show that neither overflow nor underflow can occur, we apply the occurrence count condition formulated above. Applying the condition to place p6, we get

$$n + \#(\sigma,\text{take}) - \#(\sigma,\text{dep}) \geq 0$$

Thus, $d \leq n$, and there is no buffer overflow. Applying the condition to place p5, we get

$$0 + \#(\sigma,\text{dep}) - \#(\sigma,\text{take}) \geq 0$$

Thus $d \geq 0$, and there is no underflow.

10.3.5 Verifying Producer–Consumer Systems Using LOTOS

For LOTOS-based descriptions of a variety of simple producer–consumer systems, see Reference 8. All the systems considered there deal with a buffer capacity of 1, and some are indeed a simplified version of the SCP protocol of Section 8.2.1.

We are interested in the case of a producer–consumer system (also discussed in Reference 8) that takes into account the possibility of a channel failure. This LOTOS program uses the *disable operator* [>. This operator models an interruption of a process by another process. Thus **P1[> P2** means that process **P1** may be interrupted at any point in favor of process **P2**.

The following is a LOTOS program of a producer–consumer system, with a buffer capacity of 1, that incorporates the possibility of channel failure:

File prodcons.lotos
specification prodcons[Put,Get]:noexit behaviour
      (Prod[Put] ||| Cons[Get])
      ||
      (Channel[Put,Get][>Channel_Down)

where
    process Prod[Put]:noexit:=
        Put;Prod[Put]
    endproc
    process Cons[Get]:noexit:=
    endproc
    process Channel[Put,Get]:noexit:=
        Put;Get;Channel[Put,Get]
    endproc
    process Channel_Down:noexit:=
        i;(* channel goes down *)stop
    endproc
endspec

The interpretation of the above LOTOS program becomes clear by considering the corresponding aut-file:

File prodcons.aut
des(0,6,4)
(0,Put,1)
(1,Get,3)
(3,Put,1)
(0,i,2)
(1,i,2)
(3,i,2)

10.3.6 Verification of Multiple-Producer Multiple-Consumer Systems

The system represented by the Petri net *pc.net* (see Section 10.3.2) is easily extended to the case where the required items are produced by more than one producer and/or are consumed by more than one consumer (cf. p. 65 of Reference 9). We simply extend *pc.net* by increasing the initial markings of places p1 and p3. Note that the analysis of Section 10.3.4 is easily modified accordingly!

10.3.6.1 A 2-Producer–2-Consumer System with Priority A 2-producer, 2-consumer system with priority is described in Reference 9, pp. 194–195. Another 2-producer, 2-consumer system is discussed in Reference 10, p. 546. A simplified version of the latter is presented below. This system consists of two subsystems, A and B. Each subsystem is

similar to the system represented in Section 10.3.2, but with a buffer capacity of 1. Furthermore, subsystem A has priority over subsystem B. Namely, consumer B can be active only if buffer A is empty.

File procon.net

```
.model procon.net
.inputs prodA depA takeA consA prodB depB takeB consB
.graph
#producer A
p1 prodA
prodA p2
p2 depA
depA p1
#consumer A
p4 takeA
takeA p5
p5 consA
consA p4
#producer B
p6 prodB
prodB p7
p7 depB
depB  p6
#consumer B
p9 takeB
takeB  p10
p10 consB
consB p9
#buffer A
depA p3
p3 takeA
p3 takeB (0)
takeA p11
p11 depA
#buffer B
depB p8
p8 takeB
takeB p12
p12 depB
.marking {p1 p4 p6 p9 p11 p12}
.end
```

EXERCISE

10.8   Convert the above file into an observation-equivalent specification without inhibitor arcs.

10.4   VERIFICATION BASED ON DESIGN APPROACHES

In this section we consider various approaches to the design of systems and circuits. However, within the framework of this book, we are not concerned with proving the correctness of general synthesis procedures. Instead, we wish to apply our methods of verification to examples of proposed synthesis approaches. The verification of the general synthesis procedures remains an interesting research problem.

10.4.1   Synthesis Approach #1

Let us consider circuit behavior specifications based on the Blot operators '[ ]' and '||'. Let OPj denote either of the two operators, and consider the following Blot circuit behavior specification:

$$\text{cct1.spec} = *(((a;\$ \text{ OP1 } b;\$) \text{ OP2 } (c;\$ \text{ OP3 } d;\$)) \gg z;\$)$$

10.4.1.1   Realization   We claim that the above circuit specification may be realized by the following modular circuit (Blot representation):

$$\text{cct1.imp} = (\text{MO1}[a,b,y1] \;|||\; \text{MO3}[c,d,y2]) \;||\; \text{MO2}[y1,y2,z] \backslash \{y1,y2\}$$

Here, **MOj = XOR** if **OPj = [ ]**, and **MOj = CEL,** if **OPj = ||** .

10.4.1.2   Formal Verification of the CXC-Circuit Example   We now illustrate the above general statement by the particular example where

$$\text{OP1} = \text{OP3} = \;||\; \text{ and } \text{OP2} = [\;].$$

This case was introduced as an example for a modular network, named CXC, in Section 3.5, where we used an informal approach to its verification, based on a step-by-step simulation.

We now claim that **CXC.imp** is a Type-C realization of **CXC.spec** (both are defined in Section 3.5), provided that each module is started in one of its admissible initial states. We now need to illustrate the application of our formal verification methods.

EXERCISE

10.9(a) Use LOTOS/CADP to prove that **CXC.imp** is a Type-C realization of **CXC.spec**.
   (b) Define **CXC.spec** and **CXC.imp** using CCS. Then apply CWB.NC to show the corresponding language containment.

10.4.1.3 Another Synthesis Verification Example The above synthesis approach is also easily applied to suitable extensions of the above specification constructs. As an example, consider the following Blot specification:

$$\textbf{exa\_cct.spec} = *((a;\$ \parallel (b;\$ \,[]\, c;\$) \parallel (d;\$ \,[]\, e;\$)) \gg z;\$)$$

EXERCISE

10.10(a) Construct the Blot expression **exa_cct.impl** representing an implementation of **exa_cct.spec** defined above.
   (b) Derive the corresponding LOTOS files and prove formally that
      (b/1) **exa_cct.spec** is an observation preorder (recall Section 2.7) of **exa_cct.impl**
      (b/2) **exa_cct.impl** is a Type-C realization of its specification **exa_cct.spec**
   (c) Define **exa_cct.spec** and **exa_cct.impl** using CCS, and then use CWB-NC to prove the relevant language containment.

10.4.2 Synthesis Approach #2

In this section we consider the synthesis of modular networks specified by suitably marked graphs that are realizable by **CEL** and **ICEL** modules. In the next section we extend this approach by including **XOR** modules.

Let SPN be a marked graph, viewed as specification net (see Section 7.7.5), that satisfies the following restrictions:

(1) SPN is composed of two or more cycles of length 2.
(2) Each cycle contains exactly one token.
(3) Each node of in-degree 1 is labeled by an input signal. All other nodes are labeled by output signals.

We illustrate this relevant synthesis procedure by means of the following example.

Let **SPNX1** be the following Petri net, described in PETRIFY:

File SPNX1.net
.model SPNX1.net
.inputs a b c
.outputs y z
.graph
a y
b z
c y
y a c z
z b y
.marking {<y,a> <y,c> <y,z> <z,b>}
.end

———————————

For each output, e.g., **y**, we define the subgraph consisting of all edges containing **y**. This subgraph evidently defines the module **CEL3[a,c,z,y]**. Similarly, the subgraph determined by the output **z** defines the module **ICEL[y,b,z]**. We claim that

$$\textbf{icel.net[y,b,z]} \parallel \textbf{cel3.net[a,c,z,y]} == \textbf{SPNX1.net}$$

where '$==$'denotes observation equivalence, and that consequently

ICEL[y,b,z] $\parallel$ **CEL3[a,c,z,y]** is a Type-B realization of **SPNX1**.

EXERCISE

10.11   Prove the above claim.

10.4.3   Extending the Synthesis Method by Adding XOR Modules

We show, by an example, how the above synthesis method can be extended to incorporate **XOR (MERGE)** modules. Consider the following specification net:

File xc.net
.model xc.net
.inputs a b d e
.outputs z
.graph

```
a z
b z
p1 z
p0 d e
d p1
e p1
z a b p0
.marking {<z,a> <z,b> p0}
.end
```

Note that in this example the input transitions **d**, **e** have the same input places and the same output places. Consider the net xc3 m.net obtained by merging the two input transitions **d**, **e** into a single one, say **c**. The outcome is realized by **CEL3[a,b,c,z]**. The above merging can be realized by an **XOR (MERGE)** module **XOR[d,e,c]**. The outcome of this synthesis procedure is the modular network

$$(\textbf{XOR[d,e,c]} \parallel \textbf{CEL3[a,b,c,z]}) \backslash \{\textbf{c}\}.$$

EXERCISE

10.12 Prove that the above modular network is indeed a Type-D realization of the specification net *xc.net*.

10.4.4 A Decomposition Approach

This is an alternative method for designing Type-D realizations from suitable net specifications. The specification net involved is assumed to satisfy the following requirements:

(1) The net is a labeled Petri net. The labels are of the following types:
   (a) input labels
   (b) output labels; the relevant outputs may be observable or hidden
   (c) dummy
(2) The net is safe, live, and free-choice.

A net is free-choice, if the following condition is met: If two transitions t1 and t2 share a common input place p, then p is the only input place of both t1 and t2.

The following example illustrates the above decomposition approach. It also shows how the concept of Type-D realization may be extended to networks with more than one output. The net representation of the circuit **CXC**, defined in Section 10.4.1, is as follows:

File CXC.net
.model CXC.net
.inputs a b c d
.outputs x y z
.dummy t1 t2
.graph
p0 t1 t2
t1 a b
t2 c d
a x
b x
c y
d y
x p1
y p1
p1 z
z p0
.marking {p0}
.end

It is easy to ascertain that the above net is indeed safe, live, and free-choice.

Now, we extract the following subnets, which relate inputs to outputs:

Subnet #1:
a x
b x
Subnet #2:
c y
d y
Subnet #3:
x p1
y p1
p1 z

The above subnets yield the following implementation:

$$(CEL[A,B,X] \; ||| \; CEL[C,D,Y]) \; || \; XOR[X,Y,Z]$$

EXERCISE

10.13 Prove that the preceding implementation is indeed a Type-D realization of the relevant specification net.

10.5 VERIFICATION OF TOGGLES AND TRANSITION COUNTERS

10.5.1 Verification of *k*-Toggles

We discussed the specification of k-toggles for $k=2$ in Section 7.4 and for $k>2$ in Section 7.5.

In this section we consider the design of k-toggles for arbitrary values of k, following the approach of Reference 7.

(1) If k is a power of 2, a k-toggle may be designed as a tree of 2-toggles.
(2) A $(k-1)$-toggle may be derived from a k-toggle by the inclusion of an XOR-gate and a suitable feedback connection, as illustrated in Fig. 10.4.
(3) For $k=mn$, where $m>1$ and $n>1$, a k-toggle may be implemented by means of an m-toggle, each output of which is connected to an n-toggle.

The above methods (1), (2), and (3) can be combined in several ways to obtain the design of k-toggles for arbitrary values of k. For example, using Blot, a 4-toggle may be implemented as follows:

TOG4.impl[a,y1,y2,y3,y4] =

(TOG[a,x1,x2] || (TOG[x1,y1,y3] ||| TOG[x2,y2,y4]))\{x1,x2}

Note that the design of the 3-toggle, described in Section 7.5, combines the above design methods (1) and (2).

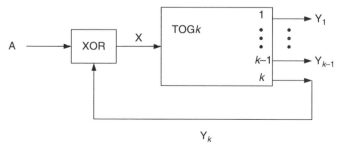

Figure 10.4 A $(k-1)$-toggle derived from a k-toggle.

EXERCISE

10.14   Assuming the 3-toggle, as specified, to be a basic building block, design an implementation of a 5-toggle. Use CADP to prove that this implementation is a Type-C realization of the corresponding specification.

10.5.2   Verification of Counters without Outputs

In the sequel we consider up–down transition counters. They count input transitions (level changes) within a given range. We denote by UP the level input whose transitions increment the count and by DOWN the level input whose transitions decrement the count. We denote by 'up' the (up- or down-) transition of UP and by 'down' any transition of DOWN.

We start by considering up–down transition counters without associating outputs that would indicate the present count state. The issue of outputs will be taken up in the next section.

Let **udcntk** denote an up–down transition counter capable of counting within the range $0-k$. The following is a state graph representing **udcnt3**; we denote the corresponding process by **Pudcnt3**, with **state$j$** represented by **Proc$j$**:

$$\textbf{udcnt3.sg} = \textbf{state0 [up > state1 [up > state2 [up > state3 [down >}$$

$$\textbf{state2 [down > state1 [down > state0}$$

It turns out that **Pudcnt3** may also be represented by

$$\textbf{udcount3} = \textbf{udc3} \setminus \{\textbf{x, y}\}$$

where **udc3** is specified as follows:

$$\textbf{udc3[up,down,x,y]} = \textbf{(*[up;x]} \parallel \textbf{*[x;y])} \parallel \textbf{*[y;down]}$$

EXERCISE

10.15   Use CADP to show that **Pudcnt3** and **udcount3** are strongly equivalent.

10.5.2.1   Direct Verification of udcount   We wish to prove directly that **udcount3** and **Pudcnt3** are indeed strongly equivalent. Let

proc0 : = **udc3**

proc1 : = *[up;x] || *[x;y] || *[down;y]

proc2 : = *[up;x] || *[y;x] || *[down;y]

proc3 : = *[x;up] || *[y;x] || *[down;y]

It is easy as verify the following:

proc0 = up;x;y;proc1

proc1 = down;proc0 [ ] up;x;proc2

proc2 = down;y;proc1 [ ] up;proc3

proc3 = down;y;x;proc2

Thus, after hiding **x** and **y**, **udc3** \ {**x,y**} becomes isomorphic to **Pudcnt3**, with **proc***j*, as specified above, corresponding to **Proc***j* of **Pudcnt3**.

10.5.2.2 Verification of udcount Using Petri Net   Next, we use PETRIFY to specify **udcount3**. The following file is a concise, non-safe representation:

File threecnt.net
.model threecnt.net
.inputs a b
.graph
p0 a
a p1
p1 b
b p0
.capacity p0 = 3 p1 = 3
.marking {p0 = 3}
.end

We may convert the above net into a state graph count3.sg by applying the command

write_sg threecnt.net -o count3.sg

The outcome is isomorphic to **udcnt3.sg** defined above.

10.5.3   Verification of Up–Down Counters with Output

The variables x, y hidden in the definition of udcount3 in Section 10.5.2 may serve to identify the various states of the counter by adding suitable output logic. Hence we define

$$\textbf{udcount3.sp[up,down,x,y]} = \textbf{udc3[up,down,x,y]}$$

$$= \textbf{*[up;x] || *[x;y] || *[y;down]}$$

Note that in Section 7.7.2 we referred to the above expression just as **spec1**. We also proved that **spec1 = impl1**, where

$$\textbf{impl1} = \textbf{udcount3.imp[up,down,x,y]} = \textbf{ICEL[y,up,x] || ICEL[down,x,y]}$$

EXERCISE

10.16   Represent **udcount3.sp** and **udcount3.imp** by labeled Petri nets. Show that the two nets are strongly equivalent.

The above considerations dealing with udcounters(k) for $k = 3$ are easily extended to higher values of k. For example, for $k = 4$, we formulate the following definitions:

$$\textbf{udcount4.sp[up,down,x,y,z]} = \textbf{*[up;x] || *[x;y] || *[y;z] || *[z;down]}$$

$$\textbf{udcount4.imp[up,down,x,y,z]} =$$

$$\textbf{ICEL[y,up,x] || ICEL[z,x,y] || ICEL[down,y,z]}$$

EXERCISE

10.17   Use PETRIFY to prove that **udcount4.sp** and **udcount4.imp** are strongly equivalent.

10.5.4   Verification of Modulo-*N* Transition Counters

In this section we introduce the concept of modulo-N transition counters, and indicate methods of synthesis, using the modules XOR and TOGGLE. This section is mainly based on Reference 11. The synthesis methods referred to in this section will be used in the sequel to illustrate our verification methods.

Modulo-N transition counters, defined below, can evidently be derived from N-toggles, with their outputs suitably relabeled. In the design approach detailed below only 2-toggles are used. This design method below is closely related to the methods of designing k-toggles, discussed in Section 10.5.1.

10.5.4.1 Specification of Modulo-N Transition Counter
A modulo-N (transition) counter can be specified as follows:

Inputs: a

Outputs: y,z

Behavior: cnt.N[a,y,z] := *[(a;y)**(N − 1);a;z]

          where w**N denotes the sequential repetition of w, N times.

For example, **cnt.3[a,y,z] = *[a;y;a;y;a;z]**.

Note that the module TOGGLE coincides with the modulo-2 transition counter.

10.5.4.2 Decompositions of Modulo-N Counters
In accordance with Reference 11, the modulo-N counter, for even $N > 2$, can be decomposed into a modulo-$N/2$ counter, a TOGGLE, and an XOR-gate, as follows:

Proposition 10.1

$$\text{cnt.}N[a,y,z] = ((\text{cnt.}N/2[a,p,q] \parallel \text{TOG}[q,x,z]) \parallel \text{XOR}[p,x,y]) \backslash \{p,q,x\}$$

For odd $N > 2$, the decomposition is as follows:

Proposition 10.2

$$\text{cnt.}N[a,y,z] = ((\text{cnt.}(N+1)/2[r,y,q] \parallel \text{TOG}[q,s,z]) \parallel \text{XOR}[a,s,r]) \backslash \{r,q,s\}$$

Furthermore, the following decomposition rule is rather evident:

Proposition 10.3   Let $N = N_1 \times N_2$, where $N_1 > 2$, $N_2 > 2$.

Then cnt.N[a,y,z] = (cnt.N_1[a,y,q] $\parallel$ cnt.N_2[q,y,z])\{q}

Rather than proving the above decomposition rules, we wish to use them for the purpose of illustrating our approaches to the formal verification of modulo-N transition counters.

10.5.4.3 Verifying a Modulo-3 Counter
Using Blot, a modulo-3 counter is specified as follows:

$$\textbf{cnt3.sp} = {}^{+}[\textbf{a;y;a;y;a;z}]$$

Its implementation is represented by the following Blot expression:

$$cnt3.impl = ((XOR[A, R3, R1] \| TOG[R1, Y, R2])$$

$$\| TOG[R2, R3, Z]) \setminus \{R1, R2, R3\}$$

EXERCISE

10.18 Use CADP to prove that **cnt3.impl** is a Type-C realization of **cnt3.sp**. *Note*: In this case, the verification of (Req C4) using the method discussed in Section 7.7.4 is not convenient. A reasonable alternative is to generate cnt3.omin. By following the (unique) sequence a;y;a;y;a;z leading from state 0 back to state 0, one immediately verifies that no undesirable output is produced.

10.5.4.4 Verifying a Modulo-12 Counter Informally, a modulo-12 counter may be specified by

$$cnt12sp = {}^*[a;y;\dots;a;y;a;z]$$

where **a;y;** is to be repeated 11 times.

One approach to the implementation of **cnt12impl** is the application of Proposition 10.3, yielding

$$cnt12impl[a, y, z] = (cnt3impl[a, y, q] \,|\, [q] \,|\, cnt4impl[q, y, z]) \setminus \{q\}.$$

To design **cnt4impl**, we may use Proposition 10.1.

EXERCISES

10.19 Construct the relevant LOTOS programs for **cnt12sp** and **cnt12impl**. Then prove that **cnt12impl** is indeed a Type-C realization of **cnt12sp**.

10.20 Design LOTOS programs for **cnt5sp** and **cnt5impl** and verify that **cnt5impl** indeed realizes **cnt5sp**.

10.21 Use CCS and CWB-NC to prove that L(**cnt3.sp**) is contained in L(**cnt3.impl**).

10.6 VENDING MACHINES VERIFICATION—REVISITED

In Chapters 2–6 we introduced simple vending machines to illustrate basic approaches to the description of digital systems. In this section we illustrate further methods of system specification, taking more advanced vending machines as running examples.

In Section 2.6 we introduced the simple vending machine **VM3**, based on the work of Milner (12). We recall its Blot specification:

$$\textbf{VM3} := \textbf{in2p;big;collect;VM3 [] in1p;little;collect;VM3}$$

The customer of this machine could either insert a 2p coin, then order and collect a big chocolate, or insert a 1p coin, then order and collect a little chocolate.

In Section 6.3 we presented the CCS version of this machine, which we repeat here:

$$\textbf{VM3\_ccs} := \textbf{in2p.big.collect.VM3\_ccs + in1p.little.collect.VM3\_ccs}$$

10.6.1 Verifying Vending Machines VeMa Using CCS

We now wish to modify the above vending machine **VM3** by providing additional facilities (cf. Reference 12). Let **VeMa1** denote the machine obtained by adding the following facilities to **VM3**:

(i) After the insertion of a 1p coin, the customer can either buy a little chocolate or insert another 1p coin and buy a big chocolate.

(ii) After the insertion of a 2p coin, the customer has the choice of one big chocolate or two little ones.

We start the task of specifying **VeMa1** by constructing the corresponding state graph, shown in Fig. 10.5.

Next, we design the relevant CCS file:

File VeMa1.ccs
proc V0 = in1p.V1 + in2p.V2
proc V1 = in1p.V3 + little.V4
proc V2 = little.V5 + big.V4
proc V3 = big.V4
proc V4 = collect.V0
proc V5 = little.V4

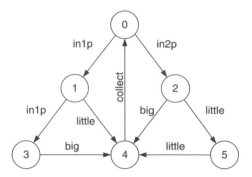

Figure 10.5 State graph of vending machine VeMa1.

Furthermore, we construct the CCS file representing the above agent:

File VM3.ccs
proc VM3 = in2p.big.collect.VM3 + in1p.little.collect.VM3

Note that V0 is the initial state of **VeMa1.ccs**. Hence the following statement, confirmed by CWB-NC, indicates that L(**VM3.ccs**) is contained in L(**VeMa1.ccs**):

le -Smay VM3 V0

EXERCISE

10.22(a) Let VeMa2 be the vending machine VM3, extended by the facility (i) specified above. Design the corresponding CCS-file VeMa2.ccs and use CWB-NC to show that L(VeMa2.ccs) is contained in L(VeMa1.ccs).

(b) Let VeMa3 be the vending machine VM3, extended by the facility (ii) specified above. Design the corresponding CCS-file VeMa3.ccs and use CWB-NC to show that L(VeMa3.ccs) is contained in L(VeMa1.ccs).

10.6.2 Verifying Vending Machines VeMa Using LOTOS

The following is a LOTOS version of **VeMa1** (with abbreviated event names):

File VeMa1.lotos
specification VeMa1[in1,in2,li,bi,co]:noexit behaviour
        VeMa1[in1,in2,li,bi,co]

where
    process VeMa1[in1,in2,li,bi,co]:noexit:=
        in1;V1[in1,in2,li,bi,co] [] in2;V2[in1,in2,li,bi,co]
    endproc
    process V1[in1,in2,li,bi,co]:noexit:=
        in1;V3[in1,in2,li,bi,co] [] li;V4[in1,in2,li,bi,co]
    endproc
    process V2[in1,in2,li,bi,co]:noexit:=
        li;V5[in1,in2,li,bi,co] [] bi;V4[in1,in2,li,bi,co]
    endproc
    process V3[in1,in2,li,bi,co]:noexit:=
        bi;V4[in1,in2,li,bi,co]
    endproc
    process V4[in1,in2,li,bi,co]:noexit:=
        co;VeMa1[in1,in2,li,bi,co]
    endproc
    process V5[in1,in2,li,bi,co]:noexit:=
        li;V4[in1,in2,li,bi,co]
    endproc
endspec

EXERCISE

10.23(a) Design a LOTOS file VM3.lotos representing VM3.
   (b) Use CADP to show that VM3 is a subsystem of VeMa1.
   (c) Design LOTOS files VeMa2.lotos and VeMa3.lotos representing the corresponding systems defined in Exercise 10.22.
   (d) Use CADP to show that VeMa2 and VeMa3 are subsystems of VeMa1.

10.7 PI-REALIZATIONS

In Section 5.16 we introduced the concept of "true concurrency", dealing with multiple events that occur simultaneously in some circuit or system. Taking true concurrency into account provides insights beyond the customary approach of replacing true concurrency by (non-deterministic) interleaving. As an illustration of this point, consider the circuit (a NAND-latch) shown in Fig. 10.6.

This circuit is in one of its stable states if $IN1 = IN2 = 0$ and $OUT1 = OUT2 = 1$. Assume that, starting from this stable state, both inputs are

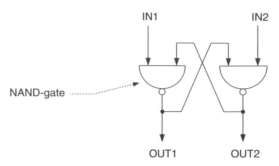

Figure 10.6 NAND-latch.

changed simultaneously, and the circuit enters the state $IN1 = IN2 = OUT1 = OUT2 = 1$. It is easy to verify that this "all-1" state causes the circuit to "oscillate", i.e., the outputs keep on changing, provided the two NAND-gates have almost equal delays. Note that this circuit behavior is not achievable if input changes are restricted to one at a time!

The above-mentioned customary approach of replacing true concurrency by interleaving also applies to the concepts of realization introduced in Chapter 7. In this section we introduce the concept of "pi-realization", which takes true concurrency into proper account. An important relevant tool is the "pi-language" of labeled Petri nets, introduced in Section 5.16.1.

10.7.1 More on Modular Networks

In Section 7.6 we briefly discussed networks formed by the "suitable" interconnection of basic modules. We now explore this concept somewhat further. We represent modular networks by means of "network diagrams". Later on we introduce a suitable algebraic notation. An example of a network diagram is shown in Fig. 10.7.

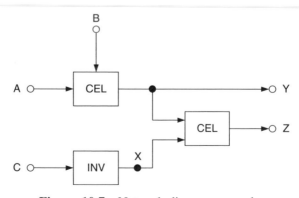

Figure 10.7 Network diagram example.

A *network diagram* is a finite directed graph with the following node types:

(a) External nodes (terminals), shown as small circles. An external node is either an "input terminal" with indegree 0 or an "output terminal" with indegree 1.

(b) Internal nodes, shown as black dots. They are hidden from an outside observer. Their indegree is 1.

  We use A, B, C to denote input terminals, Y, Z for output terminals, and X for internal nodes. Subscripts may be added if necessary.

(c) Module nodes, shown as squares with labels, identifying the type of the module, written inside the square. In particular, we use the labels INV, XOR, CEL, as introduced in Chapter 7, as well as AND, OR, NAND, defined in Section 10.1.

We say that two networks NW_1 and NW_2 are *compatible* if the following conditions are met:

(a) Any shared node label is a terminal label in both networks.

(b) Any shared node label may not be an output terminal label in both networks.

If NW_1 and NW_2 are compatible, we define their *composition* $NW_1 | NW_2$ as follows. $NW = NW_1 | NW_2$ is the interconnection of NW_1 and NW_2, obtained by identifying terminals with equal labels. If two input terminals are identified, the outcome is again an input terminal of NW. If an input terminal and an output terminal are identified, then the outcome is either an output terminal of NW or, alternatively, an internal node of NW. To cover the latter case, we apply the hiding operator '\', and use the notation $NW = (NW_1 | NW_2) \backslash$ Int, where Int denotes the set of internal nodes.

Thus the network NW shown in Fig. 10.7 may be described as follows:

$$NW = (CEL[A,B,Y] \mid INV[C,X] \mid CEL[X,Y,Z]) \backslash \{X\}$$

10.7.2 Introducing Circuits

A *state* of a network NW is an assignment of binary values (0, 1) to the external and internal nodes of NW.

A *circuit* CCT is a pair (NW,q), where q is a state of NW.

Let $CCT_i = (NW_i, q_i)$, $i = 1, 2$. CCT_1 and CCT_2 are *compatible* iff this is the case with respect to NW_1 and NW_2 and, furthermore, q_1 and q_2 are *compatible*, i.e., terminals having equal labels also have equal values.

The operator $\mid$ is extended to circuits in the evident sense.

Two networks NW_1 and NW_2 are *strongly compatible*, iff they are compatible, and furthermore, the following condition is also met:

(i) Any shared label may not be an input terminal label in both networks.

In this case we use the notation $NW_1 \# NW_2$ to denote their composition, with the hiding operator applied to all nodes obtained by identifying terminals. Thus terminals with equal labels in NW_1 and NW_2 become internal nodes of the combined network $NW_1 \# NW_2$.

The definition of '#' is extended to circuits similar to the extension of '|'.

10.7.3   Concurrent Behavior of Circuits

Let $CCT = (NW, q)$ be a circuit, where NW is represented by a network diagram. The labels of the external and internal nodes represent binary variables. We use the corresponding lower-case letters to denote the associated "signals", i.e., the relevant up- and down-transitions. We associate with NW an input signal alphabet inNW, an output signal alphabet outNW, and an internal signal alphabet intNW.

Given a state q of NW, we denote the local state of each module node in the obvious way. The node representing the output of a module (which is either an internal node or an output node of NW) is *stable* iff the corresponding module node is stable.

A state of NW is *stable* iff all its internal nodes and output terminals are stable.

Let q be a stable state of NW, and let s be a nonempty subset of inNW. Then s is applicable to state q. We write $q[s > q'$, where q' is the stable state obtained by applying s to state q.

Now let q' be an unstable state of NW, and let T denote any nonempty set of nodes, each of which is either an input node or an unstable node. Then t, the set of signals corresponding to T, is applicable to state q', and we use again the notation $q'[t > q''$.

We now proceed to define $msb(NW, q0)$, i.e., the "multiple-signal behavior" of $(NW, q0)$, for a given initial state q0 of NW.

Let $q_0, q_1, \ldots, q_n$ ($q_0 = q0$) be a sequence of states of NW, and let $t_1, \ldots, t_n$ be a sequence of signal sets, such that $q_i[t_{i+1} > q_{i+1}$ for $0 \leq i < n$. Then $q_0, t_1, q_1, \ldots, t_n, q_n$ is a *state-signal sequence* of $(NW, q0)$. Let $w = s_1, \ldots, s_m$, where $m \leq n$, be the signal-set sequence obtained from $t_1, \ldots, t_n$ by omitting all internal node signals. We again use the notation $q_0[w > q_n$. The sequence w is a *multiple-signal sequence* of (NW, q_0). The *multiple-signal behavior* $msb(NW, q_0)$ is defined as the set of all such multiple-signal sequences of (NW, q_0), including the empty sequence Λ.

As an example, we return to the network of Fig. 10.7. We shall represent a state of NW by means of the bit vector $<A,B,C,X,Y,Z>$. Let $q0 = 001000$ be the initial state of NW. The following are examples of state/signal sequences of (NW,q0):

seq1 $= <001000, \{a,b,c\}, 110000, \{x,y\}, 110110, \{z\}, 110111>$
seq2 $= <001000, \{a,b\}, 111000, \{y\}, 111010, \{a\}, 011010, \{c\}, 010010,$
$\{x\}, 010110, \{z\}, 010111>$

Therefore $<\{a,b,c\},\{y\},\{z\}>$ and $<\{a,b\},\{y\},\{a\},\{c\},\{z\}>$ are multiple-signal sequences of $CCT = (NW,q0)$.

10.7.4 Pi-Specifications of Circuits

Pi-specifications of circuits specify the concurrent (pi-) behavior of the type of circuits defined above. In order to deal with such specifications, we introduce the concept of "pi-processes".

10.7.4.1 *Pi-Processes*   Given a finite alphabet A, let ext(A) be the alphabet consisting of all nonempty subsets of A. We define a *subset language* or *pi-language* over A to be any language over ext(A). A *pi-process* P is defined as a triple $P = (inP,outP,bP)$, where inP and outP are disjoint finite alphabets and bP is a subset language over the union of inP and outP.

10.7.4.2 *Specifying Circuits by Pi-Processes*   Here we present a suitably modified version of the concept of "Type-C realization" introduced in Section 7.7.4.

If the pi-process P is to be a specification for a circuit $CCT = (NW,q0)$, we require first of all that

(**Req pi1**) $inP = inNW$ and $outP = outNW$

(**Req pi2**) bP is a subset of msb(CCT)

Furthermore, we again wish to exclude the possibility of "undesirable" outputs. We formulate this requirement as follows:

(**Req pi3**) If w is a sequence in bP, x is a subset of outP, and the concatenation w;x is a sequence in msb(CCT), then w;x is also a sequence in bP.

The following requirement takes into consideration the possibility of non-deterministic circuit behavior:

(**Req pi4**) If w;w' is a sequence in bP, and q is a state of NW reachable from the initial state q0 of CCT by applying w, i.e., q0[w > q, then w' is applicable to state q, i.e., q[w' > q' for some state q' of NW.

If all four requirements are satisfied then we say that the circuit CCT *satisfies* P, denoted by CCT |= P.

10.7.5 Simple Verification Examples

We shall replace, whenever convenient, a singleton set by its unique element. Also, we shall write, e.g., abz for $<$a,b,z$>$.

Example piX1 Let P1 = ({a,b},{z},{abz}) and CCT1 = (AND[A,B,Z], 000). Clearly, CCT1|= P1, since $<$000, a, 100, b, 110, z, 111$>$ is a state/ signal sequence of CCT1. However, P1 has also a simpler realization. For example

$$CCT2 = ((WIRE[A,X] \;||\; WIRE[B,Z])\backslash\{X\}, 0000)$$

where the initial (stable) states of [A,Z] are A = Z. We evidently have CCT2 |= P1.

Now let P2 = ({a,b},{z},{a,b,abz}). We still have CCT1 |= P2, but CCT2 |= P2 does not hold. Indeed, requirement (Req pi3) is not satisfied: $<$b$>$ is a sequence belonging to both b(P2) and msb(CCT2), $<$b,z$>$ is in msb(CCT2), but is not in b(P2).

10.7.6 Applying Net Algebra

In Section 5.12 we introduced an algebraic approach to the description of Petri nets. Here we recall the main concepts. We shall use the letter H, with or without subscripts, to denote an algebraic description of a labeled Petri net.

H_a, H_b, H_c, and H_d, defined as follows, are examples of such descriptions:

(a) H_a = a;{} [] b;{}
(b) H_b = [a;b;{}]
(c) H_c = *[a;b]
(d) H_d = [a;c;{}] || [b;c;{}]

The graphical representations of the corresponding labeled nets are shown in Fig. 10.8.

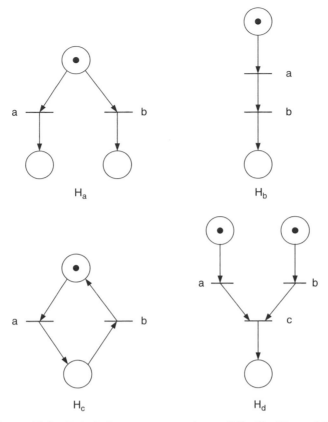

Figure 10.8   Labeled net representations of H_a, H_b, H_c, and H_d.

We define an *entry place* of a net as a place without input transitions and with at least one output transition. An *exit place* of a net is defined similarly.

A *1-1 net* has exactly one entry place and exactly one exit place and no isolated places.

Let H_1 and H_2 be 1-1 nets. Then $H_1 \& H_2$ denotes the 1-1 net illustrated in Fig. 10.9 for $[a;\{\} \& b;\{\}]$.

Furthermore, the net $H_1 \# H_2$ is derived from $H_1 \parallel H_2$ by replacing with λ the label of any transition that has been obtained by identifying equally labeled transitions of H_1 and H_2.

10.7.7 Another Verification Example

Recall the definition of labeled nets introduced in Section 5.5. A labeled net $LPN = (PN, \Sigma, lb)$ is a *specification net* iff Σ is partitioned into an *input alphabet* inLPN and an *output alphabet* outLPN. We associate the

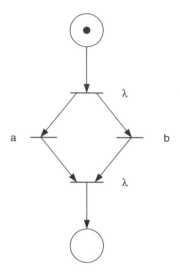

Figure 10.9   1-1 net representation of [a;{} & b;{}].

pi-process P(LPN) = (inLPN,outLPN,pi(LPN)) with a specification net LPN. In this case we write CCT |= LPN instead of CCT |= P(LPN).

Example piX2   Let

$$CCT1 = (CEL[A,B,Y], 000)$$

$$CCT2 = (CEL[Y,C,Z],000)$$

$$H1 = *[a;y] \| *[b;y], inH1 = \{a,b\}, outH1 = \{y\}$$

$$H2 = *[y;z] \| *[c;z], inH2 = \{y,c\}, outH2 = \{z\}$$

Then

$$(a)\ CCT1\#CCT2 |= H1\#H2$$

But

$$(b)\ CCT1|CCT2 |= H1 \| H2\ does\ not\ hold$$

EXERCISE

10.24   Prove the statements (a) and (b) from Example piX2.

10.7.8 Some Pi Propositions

The following are some propositions relating specification nets to their pi-realizations:

Proposition Pi1 Consider the following specification net:

$$HC_n = *[a_0;z] \| \ldots \| *[a_n;z], \, n > 0$$

where

$$inHC_n = \{a_0, \ldots, a_n\}$$

and

$$outHC_n = \{z\}$$

Let NC_n, $n > 0$, be a cascade connection of n two-input C-elements, defined inductively as follows:

$$NC_1 = CEL[A_0, A_1, Z_1]$$

$$NC_n = NC_{n-1} \, \# \, CEL[Z_{n-1}, A_n, Z]$$

Let q0 be one of the two states of NC_n, in which all the input, output, and internal variables have the same value (i.e., all are 0 or all are 1). Then

$$CCT \models P$$

where

$$CCT = (NC_n, q0)$$

and

$$P = (inHC_n, outHC_n, pi(HC_n))$$

Proof The main point is to prove requirement (Req pi2), i.e., bP is a subset of msb(CCT). In the initial marking of HC_n all input nodes (i.e., nodes labeled by input signals) are firable. All of them have to be fired, in any (sequential/parallel) order, for the output node z to become firable. After the firing of z, the initial marking is again reached. In CCT all input signals are applicable in any (sequential/parallel) order. After all of them have been applied, the output Z becomes unstable. Hence the output Z changes its value and the circuit CCT returns to one of its two initially admissible values. It follows that any multiple-firing sequence of P also belongs to msb(CCT). Thus the requirement (Req pi2) is indeed satisfied. It is easily to verify that the requirements (Req pi1), (Req pi3), and (Req pi4) are also met.

10.8   A COMPARISON OF EQUIVALENCE RELATIONS

In Section 5.16 we introduced the concept of pi-equivalence of labeled nets, and illustrated the difference between pi-equivalence and L-equivalence. In this section we discuss some conditions under which the two equivalences coincide. The treatment is mainly based on work by Wolfsthal and Yoeli (13).

In Chapter 5 we introduced the concept of labeled nets (Section 5.5) as well as that of marked graphs (Section 5.11). In this section we are concerned with the combination of both concepts, i.e., labeled marked graphs. Furthermore, we consider a restriction imposed on labeled marked graphs, namely we assume that they are "structurally deterministic (s.d.)." The definition of this concept is as follows (see Reference 14):

Definition of s.d.   Let $LPN = (PN, \Sigma, lb)$ be a labeled net, where $PN = (P, T, F)$ (see Section 5.1.3) and let M be its initial marking. LPN is *structurally deterministic* if the following conditions hold:

  (i) If the marking M' is reachable from M, t1 and t2 are transitions enabled by M', and $lb(t1) = lb(t2)$, then $t1 = t2$.
  (b) If M' is reachable from M, t is a transition enabled by M', and $lb(t) = \lambda$, then no other transition is enabled by M'.

10.8.1   An Equivalence Theorem

Theorem   Let LMG1 and LMG2 be two structurally deterministic (s.d.) labeled marked graphs. Then $pi(LMG1) = pi(LMG2)$ iff $L(LMG1) = L(LMG2)$.

Proof   For a detailed proof of this theorem, see Reference 13.

The structural determinism requirement is crucial to the validity of this Equivalence Theorem, as can be seen from the following example. We already saw in Section 5.16.2 an example of two nets that are L-equivalent but are not pi-equivalent. For another example of such a case, consider the labeled marked graphs LMG_1 and LMG_2 from Fig. 10.10. It is easily seen that $L(LMG_1) = L(LMG_2) = Pref(\{aab\}*)$, so these labeled graphs are L-equivalent. However, the word $\{a\}\{b\}$ belongs to $pi(LMG_2)$, but not to $pi(LMG_1)$, so they are not pi-equivalent. Only LMG_2 is able to perform $\{a\}\{b\}$, while LMG_1 cannot. (In $pi(LMG_2)$ this word corresponds to the concurrent firing of the two transitions labeled a, followed by the firing of the transition labeled b.)

Indeed, LMG_2 does not have the s.d.-property.

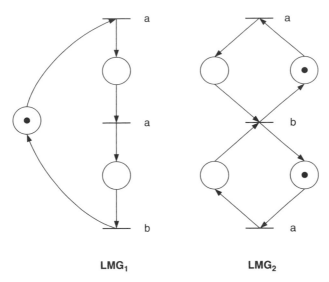

$$\textbf{LMG}_1 \qquad\qquad \textbf{LMG}_2$$

Figure 10.10 Labeled marked graphs, $L(\text{LMG}_1) = L(\text{LMG}_2)$, $\text{pi}(\text{LMG}_1) \neq \text{pi}(\text{LMG}_2)$.

10.8.2 An Application of the Equivalence Theorem

If we wish to compare two digital systems, pi-equivalence is of course a more interesting aspect than L-equivalence. However, in the general case the proof of pi-equivalence is much more difficult than the proof of L-equivalence. On the other hand, if the conditions of the above Equivalence Theorem apply, it is sufficient to check for L-equivalence in order to prove pi-equivalence.

As an example, consider the parallel system discussed in Section 7.9. In particular, refer to the marked graphs representing the specification and the implementation of the system. As stated in Section 7.9, the two graphs are L-equivalent. Since both graphs meet the condition of the Equivalence Theorem, it follows that they are also pi-equivalent.

A direct proof of pi-equivalence would require much more work! This example can easily be extended to a system controlling the concurrent performance of three or more devices.

10.9 SELECTED SOLUTIONS

10.1 The required file is as follows:

File NAND2.lotos
specification NAND2[IN1,IN2,OUT]:noexit
library BOOLEAN endlib

```
behaviour
        NAND2[IN1,IN2,OUT]
where
   process NAND2[IN1,IN2,OUT]:noexit:=
        (IN1 ?x:Bool;
        IN2 ?y:Bool;
        OUT! (not(x and y));
        NAND2[IN1,IN2,OUT])
        []
        (IN2 ?y:Bool;
        IN1 ?x:Bool;
        OUT! (not(y and x));
        NAND2[IN1,IN2,OUT])
   endproc
endspec
```

Now apply CADP as illustrated in previous examples, to show that NAND1.aut and NAND2.aut are indeed observation-equivalent.

10.2 The LOTOS file corresponding to the Boolean expression $\sim(\sim$IN1 $\vee \sim$IN2$)$ is as follows:

File ANDcomp.lotos
```
specification ANDcomp[in1,in2,out]:noexit
library BOOLEAN endlib
behaviour
        ANDcomp[in1,in2,out]
where
   process ANDcomp[in1,in2,out]:noexit:=
        ANDcomp0[in1,in2,out] >> ANDcomp[in1,in2,out]
   endproc
   process ANDcomp0[in1,in2,out]:exit:=
        hide out1, out2, out3 in
        ((NOT0[in1,out1] ||| NOT0[in2,out2]) |[out1,out2]|
        OR[out1,out2,out3]) |[out3]| NOT0[out3,out]
   endproc
```

```
    process NOT0[IN1,OUT]:exit:=
        IN1 ?x:Bool;
        OUT! not(x);
        exit
    endproc
    process  OR[IN1,IN2,OUT]:exit:=
        (IN1 ?x:Bool;exit(x,any Bool)
        |||
        IN2 ?y:Bool;exit(any Bool,y))
        >>
        accept x,y:Bool in  (OUT! (x or y); exit)
    endproc
endspec
```

Now proceed as in the previous examples to show that ANDcomp.aut and ANDgate.aut are observation-equivalent.

10.3   The two files are as follows; proceed as previously explained:

File XOR3comp.lotos
```
specification XOR3comp[in1,in2,in3,out]:noexit
library BOOLEAN endlib
behaviour
        XOR3comp[in1,in2,in3,out]
where
    process XOR3comp[in1,in2,in3,out]:noexit:=
        XOR3comp0[in1,in2,in3,out] >>XOR3comp[in1,in2,in3,out]
    endproc
    process XOR3comp0[in1,in2,in3,out]:exit:=
        hide out1 in
        XORgate[in1,in2,out1] | [out1] | XORgate[out1,in3,out]
    endproc
    process XORgate[IN1,IN2,OUT]:exit:=
        (IN1 ?x:Bool;exit(x,any Bool)
        |||
        IN2 ?y:Bool;exit(any Bool,y))
        >>
        accept x,y:Bool in  (OUT! (x xor y); exit)
    endproc
endspec
```

File XOR3gate.lotos
specification XOR3gate[IN1,IN2,IN3,OUT]:noexit
library BOOLEAN endlib
behaviour
        XOR3gate[IN1,IN2,IN3,OUT]
where
    process XOR3gate [IN1,IN2,IN3,OUT]:noexit:=
        (IN1 ?x:Bool;exit(x,any Bool,any Bool)
        |||
        IN2 ?y:Bool;exit(any Bool,y,any Bool)
        |||
        IN3 ?z:Bool;exit(any Bool,any Bool,z))
        >>
        accept x,y,z:Bool in OUT!((x xor y)xor z);
        XOR3gate[IN1,IN2,IN3,OUT]
    endproc
endspec

10.4(b)   Convert the two relevant LOTOS files into aut-files and then show that the two aut-files are indeed strongly equivalent.

10.5(a)   See Figure 10 of Reference 1.
(b)   2LCUsp = (*[rin;ain] || *[ain;rint]) || (*[ain;rint] || [*[rint;aint]) ||
              (*[rint;aint] || *[aint;rout]) || (*[aint;rout] || *[rout;aout])
          = ICEL[rin,rint,ain] || ICEL[ain,aint,rint] || ICEL[rint,rout,aint] ||
          ICEL[aint,aout,rout]

10.6   The main part of the required proof, namely a LOTOS file representing

$$\textbf{PC24ver} = \textbf{PC24imp} \,\|\, \textbf{PC24spec}$$

is as follows:

File PC24ver.lotos
specification PC24ver[a,b,y,z]:noexit behaviour
        hide x in
        (XOR(b,x,a] | [x] | TOG[z,x,y]) | [a,b,y,z] | CY[a,b,y,z]
where
(* PC24imp *)
    process XOR[ab,z]:noexit:=
        a;z;XOR[a,b,z] [] b;z;XOR[a,b,z]

```
        endproc
        process TOG[a,y,z]:noexit:=
            a;y;a;z;TOG[a,y,z]
        endproc
        (* PC24spec *)
        process CY[a,b,y,z]:noexit:=
            b;a;z;a;z;y;CY[a,b,y,z]
        endproc
    endspec
```

From this file, extract the LOTOS description of **PC24spec**. Then generate the aut-files corresponding to *PC24ver.lotos* and *PC24spec.lotos* and verify that the two aut-files are observation-equivalent.

10.7 Here again is the main part of the required proof. Let

$$\textbf{PC42ver = PC42imp} \parallel \textbf{PC42spec}$$

The relevant LOTOS file is as follows:

File PC42ver.lotos
```
specification PC42ver[a,b,y,z]:noexit behaviour
        hide x1,x2 in
        (TOG[a,b,x1] | [b,x1] | (CEL[x1,y,x2] | [x2] | XOR[b,x2,z]))
        | [a,b,y,z] |
        PC42sp[a,b,y,z]
where
    process TOG[a,y,z]:noexit:=
        a;y;a;z;TOG[a,y,z]
    endproc
    process CEL[a,b,z]:noexit:=
        a;b;z;CEL[a,b,z] [] b;a;z;CEL[a,b,z]
    endproc
    process XOR[a,b,z]:noexit:=
        a;z;XOR[a,b,z] [] b;z;XOR[a,b,z]
    endproc
    process PC42sp[a,b,y,z]:noexit:=
        a;b;z;(a;exit ||| y;exit)>>z;exit
                    >>PC42sp[a,b,y,z]
    endproc
endspec
```

From this file, extract the LOTOS description of **PC42spec**. Then generate the aut-files corresponding to *PC42ver.lotos* and *PC42spec.lotos* and verify that the two aut-files are observation-equivalent.

10.8 Apply the command (see PETRIFY Manual) *petrify -bisim procon.net*.

10.9(a) The LOTOS file representing the parallel composition of **CXC.spec** and **CXC.imp** is as follows:

File CXCver.lotos
specification CXCver[A,B,C,D,Z]:noexit behaviour
        hide y1,y2 in
        (
        ((CEL[A,B,Y1] ||| CEL[C,D,Y2])
        | [Y1,Y2] |
        XOR[Y1,Y2,Z])
        | [A,B,C,D,Z] |
        CXCSPEC[A,B,C,D,Z]
)
    where
        process CEL[A,B,Z]:noexit:=
            A;B;Z;CEL[A,B,Z] [] B;A;Z;CEL[A,B,Z]
        endproc
        process XOR[A,B,Z]:noexit:=
            A;Z;XOR[A,B,Z] [] B;Z;XOR[A,B,Z]
        endproc
        process CXCspec[A,B,C,D,Z]:noexit:=
            (A;exit ||| B;exit) [] (C;exit ||| D;exit)
                    >> Z;exit >>
            CXCspec[A,B,C,D,Z]
        endproc
    endspec

Proving (**Req C1**), (**Req C2**), and (**Req C3**) is straightforward. (**Req C4**) is best proven by direct verification. (**Req C5**) follows from (**Req C2**) (see Chapter 7).

(b) The files *cxcspec.ccs* and *cxcimpl.ccs* are as follows:

File cxcspec.ccs
proc cxcspec = a.b.z.cxcspec + b.a.z.cxcspec + c.d.z.cxcspec +
                d.c.z.cxcspec

File cxcimpl.ccs

proc cell = a.b.'y1.cell + b.a.'y1.cell
proc cel2 = c.d.'y2.cel2 + d.c.'y2.cel2
proc xor = y1.z.xor + y2.z.xor
proc cxcimp = (cell | cel2 | xor)\{y1,y2}

Enter the above two files into your CWB-NC system and issue the command

le -Smay cxcspec cxcimp

You will obtain 'TRUE'.

10.10(a)   **exa_cct.impl = ((xor[b,c,w] | [w] | cel[a,w,x]) ||| xor[d,e,y])**

| [x,y] | cel[x,y,z] \{w,x,y}

(b)

File exacct_spec.lotos

specification exacct_spec[a,b,c,d,e,z]:noexit behaviour
        exacct_spec[a,b,c,d,e,z]
where
    process exacct_spec[a,b,c,d,e,z]:noexit:=
        (((a;exit ||| (b;exit [] c;exit)) ||| (d;exit [] e;exit)
                >> z;exit) >> exacct_spec[a,b,c,d,e,z])
    endproc
endspec

File exacct_impl.lotos

specification exacct_impl[a,b,c,d,e,z]:noexit behaviour
        hide w,x,y in
        ((xor[b,c,w] | [w] | cel[w,a,x]) ||| xor[d,e,y])
        | [x,y] |
        cel[x,y,z]
where
    process xor[a,b,z]:noexit:=
        a;z;xor[a,b,z] [] b;z;xor[a,b,z]
    endproc

```
    process cel[a,b,z]:noexit:=
        a;b;z;cel[a,b,z] [] b;a;z;cel[a,b,z]
    endproc
endspec
```

(b/1)   Produce the corresponding *.aut-files and apply the command (see Section 4.10!)

aldebaran -oord file1.aut file2.aut

You will obtain 'TRUE'.

(b/2)   This is now easy! (use b/1 !).

(c)   The CCS specifications of **exacct.spec** and **exacct.impl** are as follows:

File exacctspec.ccs
proc exacct = a.b.d.z.exacct + a.b.e.z.exacct + a.c.d.z.exacct
                    + a.c.e.z.exacct

File exacctimpl.ccs
proc xor1 = b.'w.xor1 + c.'w.xor1
proc cel1 = w.a.'x.cel1 + a.w.'x.cel1
proc xor2 = d.'y.xor2 + e.'y.xor2
proc cel2 = x.y.z.cel2 + y.x.z.cel2
proc IMP = (((xor1 | cel1) | xor2) | cel2)\{w,x,y}

Now proceed as indicated in the above solution for Exercise 10.9.

10.11   A PETRIFY representation of the corresponding implementation is as follows:

File ex10_11.net
.model ex10_11.net
.inputs a b c
.outputs y z
.graph
#cel3[a,c,z,y]
a y
c y
z y
y a c z

#completing icel[y,b,z]
b z
z b
.marking {<y,a><y,c><y,z><z,b>}
.end

By applying PETRIFY to the above net, we obtain a net that coincides with the specification net **SPNX1**. This evidently completes the required proof.

10.13   The corresponding env.SPnet is as follows (see Section 7.7.5):

File cxcver.net
.model cxcver.net
.inputs a b c d
.outputs x y z
.dummy t1 t2
.graph
#cel[a,b,x]
a x
b x
x a b
#cel[c,d,y]
c y
d y
y c d
#xor[x,y,z]
p0 x y
x p1
y p1
p1 z
z p0
#env
z p2
p2 t1 t2
t1 a b
t2 c d
.marking {<x,a> <x,b> <y,c> <y,d> p0 p2}
.end

Applying PETRIFY to the above cxcver.net, we obtain a net that essentially coincides with the given specification net. It is easy to complete the proof that the above implementation is indeed a Type-D realization of the given specification net (extended to the case of multiple outputs).

10.14   Applying Blot, the required implementation may be designed as follows:

$$\textbf{TOG5.impl}[a,y1,y2,y3,y4,y5] =$$

$$(\textbf{TOG3}[b,x1,x2,x3] \,\|\, (\textbf{TOG}[x1,y1,y4] \,\|\|\|$$

$$\textbf{TOG}[x2,y2,y5] \,\|\|\| \,\textbf{TOG}[x3,y3,w])$$

$$\|\, \textbf{XOR}[a,w,b]) \setminus \{b,w,x1,x2,x3\}$$

The main point of the verification is the proof that **TOG5.ver = TOG5.impl** $\|$ **TOG5.sp** and **TOG5.sp** = *[a;y1;...a;y5] are observation-equivalent. The above Blot definitions are easily converted into LOTOS files, which can be used to complete the required verification.

10.16   *File udcount3sp.net*
.model udcount3sp.net
.inputs a b
.outputs y z
.graph
*[a;y]
a y
y a
*[y;z]
y z
z y
*[z;b]
z b
b z
.marking {<y,a> <z,y> <b,z>}
.end

File udcount3imp.net
.model udcount3imp.net
.inputs a b

.outputs y z
.graph
\# ice1[z,a,y]
z y
a y
y a z
\# ice1[b,y,z]
b z
z b
\# note that the entry (z y b) is redundant
.marking { <z,y> <y,a> <b,z> }
.end

The two nets are evidently strongly equivalent.

10.18   (Partial Solution) A LOTOS file representing **cnt3.impl** is as follows:

File mod3count.lotos
specification mod3count[A,Y,Z]:noexit behaviour
   mod3count[A,Y,Z]
where
  process mod3count[A,Y,Z]:noexit:=
   hide R1,R2,R3 in
   ((XOR[A,R3,R1] | [R1] | TOG[R1,Y,R2]) | [R2,R3] |
   TOG[R2,R3,Z])
  endproc
  process XOR[A,B,Z]:noexit:=
   A;Z;XOR[A,B,Z]
   []
   B;Z;XOR[A,B,Z]
  endproc
  process TOG[A,Y,Z]:noexit:=
   A;Y;A;Z;TOG[A,Y,Z]
  endproc
endspec

---

cnt3sp is represented in the following LOTOS file:

File mod3count_sp.lotos
specification mod3count_sp[A,Y,Z]:noexit behaviour
   Q[A,Y,Z]

where
    process Q[A,Y,Z]:noexit:=
        A;Y;A;Y;A;Z;Q[A,Y,Z]
    endproc
endspec

It is now rather straightforward to prove that requirements (**Req C1**), (**Req C2**), and (**Req C3**) of Section 7.7.4 are satisfied. As to (**Req C4**), see the formulation guidelines given in the exercise itself.

10.19 (Partial Solution) The LOTOS file representing **mod12count** is as follows; use this file to complete the required verification:

File mod12count.lotos
specification mod12count[A,Y,Z]:noexit behaviour
        hide Q in
        (mod3count[A,Y,Q] | [Q] | mod4count[Q,Y,Z])
where
    process mod3count[A,Y,Z]:noexit:=
        hide R1,R2,R3 in
        ((XOR[A,R3,R1] | [R1] | TOG[R1,Y,R2]) | [R2,R3] |
        TOG[R2,R3,Z])
    endproc
    process mod4count[A,Y,Z]:noexit:=
        hide Q1,Q2,Q3 in
        ((TOG[A,Q1,Q2] | [Q2] | TOG[Q2,Q3,Z]) | [Q1,Q3] |
        XOR[Q1,Q3,Y])
    endproc
endspec

10.20 The major part of the required solution, namely a LOTOS program specifying the parallel connection of **mod5count** (=**mod5impl**) and **mod5count_sp** (=**mod5sp**), is as follows; this parallel connection and **mod5sp** are evidently equivalent:

File mod5count_ver.lotos
specification mod5count_ver[A,Y,Z]:noexit behaviour
        mod5count[A,Y,Z] || mod5count_sp[A,Y,Z]
where
    process mod5count[A,Y,Z]:noexit:=
        hide R1,R2,R3 in

```
((mod3count[R1,Y,R2] | [R2] | TOG[R2,R3,Z]) | [R1,R3] |
    XOR[A,R3,R1])
endproc
process mod3count[A,Y,Z]:noexit:=
    hide R1,R2,R3 in
    ((XOR[A,R3,R1] | [R1] | TOG[R1,Y,R2]) | [R2,R3] |
        TOG[R2,R3,Z])
endproc
process mod5count_sp[A,Y,Z]:noexit:=
    A;Y;A;Y;A;Y;A;Y;A;Z;mod5count_sp[A,Y,Z]
endproc
endspec
```

10.21 The CCS-file **cnt3.ccs** representing **cnt3.impl** and the file **cnt3sp.ccs** representing **cnt3.sp** are as follows:

File cnt3.ccs
```
proc xor = a.'r1.xor + r3.'r1.xor
proc tog1 = r1.y.r1.'r2.tog1
proc tog2 = r2.'r3.r2.z.tog2
proc cnt3 = ((xor | tog1) | tog2)\{r1,r2,r3}
```

File cnt3sp.ccs
```
proc cnt3sp = a.y.a.y.a.z.cnt3sp
```

Now load the above two files into your CWB-NC system and issue the command

le -Smay cnt3sp cnt3

You will obtain 'TRUE'.

10.10 REFERENCES

1. Sutherland IE. Micropipelines. Commun ACM 1989;32:720–738.
2. Clark G, Taylor G. The verification of asynchronous circuits using CCS. University of Edinburgh, Department of Computer Science, Technical Report ECS-LFCS-97-369, 1997.

3. Day P, Woods JV. Investigation into micropipeline latch design styles. IEEE Trans VLSI Syst 1995;3(2):264–272.

4. Furber SB, Day P. Four-phase micropipeline latch control circuits. IEEE Trans VLSI Syst 1996;4(2):247–253.

5. Taylor GS, Blair GM. Reduced complexity two-phase micropipeline latch controller. ESSCIRC' 97, September 1997.

6. Yun KY, Beerel PA, Arceo J. High-performance asynchronous pipeline circuits. In: Proceedings of International Symposium on Advanced Research in Asynchronous Circuits and Systems, April 1996.

7. Encyclopedia of Delay-Insensitive Systems (EDIS), November 1998. http://edis.win.tue.nl/

8. Logrippo L, Faci M, Haj-Hussein M. An introduction to LOTOS. Learning by Examples, 1992.

9. Peterson JL. Petri net theory and the modeling of systems. Prentice-Hall, 1981.

10. Murata T. Petri nets: properties, analysis and applications. Proc IEEE 1989;77:541–580.

11. Ebergen JC, Peters AMG. Modulo-N counters. In: Staunstrup J, Sharp R editors. Designing correct circuits. Elsevier; 1992. p 27–46.

12. Milner R. Communication and concurrency. Prentice-Hall, 1989.

13. Wolfsthal Y, Yoeli M. An equivalence theorem for labeled marked graphs. IEEE Trans Parallel Distrib Syst. 1994;5(8):886–891.

14. Yoeli M, Etzion T. Behavioral equivalence of concurrent systems. In: Applications and theory of Petri nets. Informatik-Fachberichte 66. Springer, 1983.

## CHAPTER 11

Guide to Further Studies

In this chapter we provide references to examples on applying the verification methods described in this book to very large as well as more complicated systems. We also refer to colored Petri nets, which are a powerful extension of Petri nets.

11.1 VERIFICATION OF TELECOMMUNICATION SYSTEMS

11.1.1 Plain Old Telephone System (POTS)

A Plain Old Telephone System (POTS) is a well-documented automatic (dialing-based) conventional telephone switching system. It applies the usual set of tones, i.e., dial-tone, ring-tone, busy-tone, and error-tone. The following are some examples of basic requirements:

1. It is always possible for every subscriber to lift the receiver (if in the "onhook" state) and replace it (if in the "offhook" state).
2. A subscriber, after obtaining a dial-tone, may dial any subscriber.
3. For a given subscriber, only one tone may be activated at any one time.
4. The system is deadlock-free.

For the application of Full LOTOS to the specification of examples of POTS, see Reference 1. These demos also deal with the verification of some requirements, similar to those listed above.

For additional LOTOS-based descriptions of POTS, see References 2 and 3.

Verification of Systems and Circuits Using LOTOS, Petri Nets, and CCS, by Michael Yoeli and Rakefet Kol
Copyright © 2008 John Wiley & Sons, Inc.

11.1.2   Advanced Telephone Systems

Modern telephone systems provide many facilities, much beyond those offered by POTS. Such facilities include call-forwarding, call-waiting (camp-on-busy), abbreviated dialing, outgoing call screening, and many others.

For LOTOS-oriented descriptions of advanced telephone systems, see, e.g., Reference 4. This, however, only presents fragments of Full LOTOS specifications.

In advanced systems the various features provided are likely to interfere with each other. The topic of such feature interactions is presently of considerable interest. For three such studies, based on LOTOS, see References 5–7.

11.1.3   ISDN Telephony

ISDN (Integrated Services Digital Network) involves the digitization of the telephone network, permitting the transmission of voice, data, graphics, music, and video over existing telephone wires.

For a LOTOS-oriented insight into some services provided by ISDN, see Reference 8.

11.2   VERIFICATION USING COLORED PETRI NETS

Colored Petri nets form a powerful extension of the basic Petri net concept introduced in earlier chapters. Introductory information can be found in Reference 9, and analysis methods and practical use of colored Petri nets are described in detail in Reference 10. For examples of applications, see also Reference 11, where advanced ("intelligent") telecommunication networks are discussed.

11.3   VERIFICATION OF TRAFFIC SIGNAL CONTROL SYSTEMS

In this section we refer to two papers dealing with the application of Petri nets to the modeling and analysis of traffic signal control systems.

List and Cetin (12) use Petri nets to model and analyze an eight-phase signal controller of an urban intersection. In particular, the Petri net model is intended to demonstrate how the traffic operation safety rules are enforced.

DiCesare et al. (13) use colored Petri nets to model and analyze networks of interconnected intersection controls.

11.4 REFERENCES

1. Plain Old Telephony System (POTS) demo_14 and demo_15 from CADP on-line demo examples, 2006. http://www.inrialpes.fr/vasy/cadp/demos.html.

2. Faci M, Logrippo L, Stepien B. Formal specifications of telephone systems in LOTOS. In: Protocol Specification, Testing, and Verification IX; 1989 June 6–9; Enschede, The Netherlands: North-Holland; p 25–34.

3. Faci M, Logrippo L. Stepien B. Formal specifications of telephone systems in LOTOS, the constraint-oriented style approach. Computer Networks ISDN Syst 1991;23(5):53–67.

4. Faci M, Logrippo L, Stepien B. Structural models for specifying telephone systems. Computer Networks ISDN Syst 1997;29(4):501–507.

5. Korver H. Detecting feature interactions with CAESAR/ALDEBARAN. Sci Comput Programming, July 1997. http://www.inrialpes.fr/vasy/cadp/case-studies/96-e-featureinteract.html.

6. Kamoun J, Logrippo L. Goal-oriented feature interaction detection in the intelligent network model. In: Kimbler K, Bouma LG, editors. Feature interactions in telecommunications and software systems V. IOS Press; 1998. p 172–186.

7. Fu Q, Harnois P, Logrippo L, Sincennes J. Feature interaction detection: a LOTOS-based approach. Computer Networks 2000;32(4):433–448. http://www.inrialpes.fr/vasy/cadp/case-studies/00-e-feature.html.

8. ISDN telephony teleservice and call waiting. Case Study Using CADP, 1994. http://www.inrialpes.fr/vasy/cadp/case-studies/94-c-isdn.html.

9. Jensen K. An introduction to the practical use of coloured Petri nets. In: Lectures on Petri nets II: Applications. Lecture Notes in Computer Science, 1998; 1492:237–292.

10. Jensen K. Coloured Petri nets. Springer, 1997.

11. Examples of industrial use of coloured Petri nets (CP-nets). Protocols and Networks, March 2007. http://www.daimi.au.dk/CPnets/intro/1.html.

12. List GF, Cetin M. Modeling traffic signal control using Petri nets. IEEE Trans Intell Transport Syst 2004;5(3):177–187.

13. DiCesare F, Kulp PT , Gile M, List G. The application of Petri nets to the modeling, analysis and control of intelligent urban traffic networks. Lecture Notes in Computer Science, 1994;815:2–15.

INDEX

Verification of Systems and Circuits Using LOTOS, Petri Nets, and CCS, by
Michael Yoeli and Rakefet Kol
Copyright © 2008 John Wiley & Sons, Inc.